GENT NEXT DOOR

The Secret Of Using Authentic Style, To Attract The Work, Relationship, And Life You Desire

GENT NEXT DOOR

First edition. September 13, 2020.

Copyright © 2020 Tinashe Dennis Immanuel.

ISBN: 978-1393911135

Written by Tinashe Dennis Immanuel.

Table of Contents

Tinashe Dennis Immanuel

TINASHE DENNIS IMMANUEL

GENT NEXT DOOR

"Style with Purpose!"

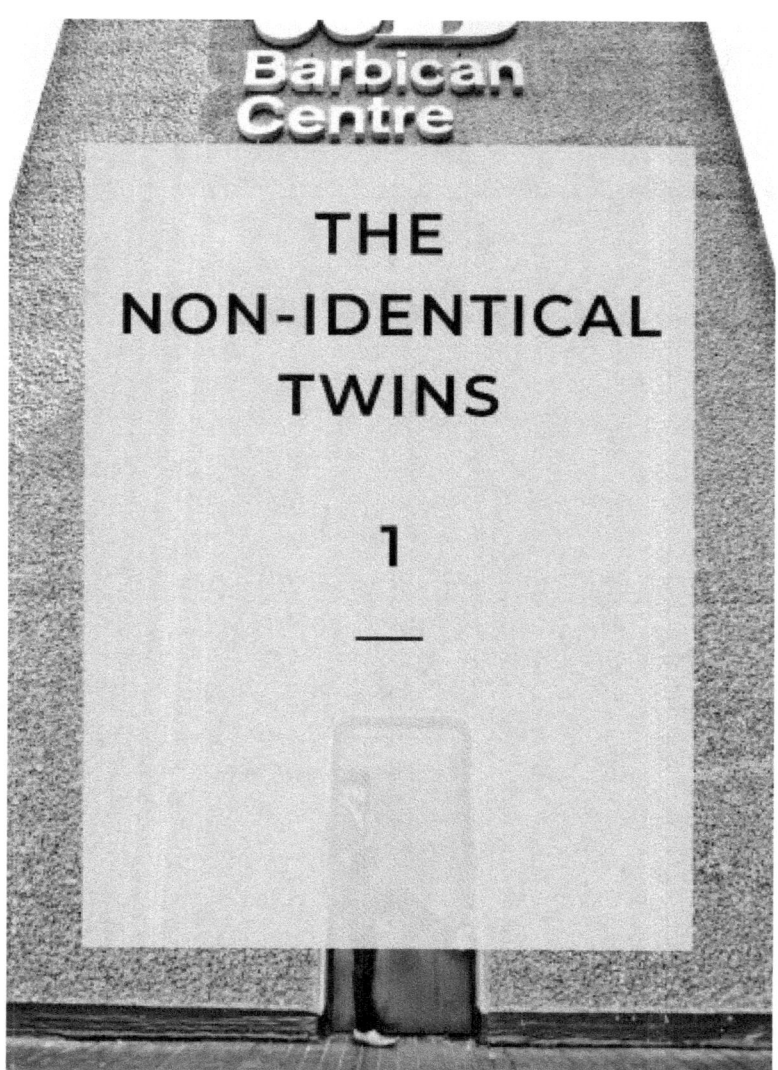

THE
NON-IDENTICAL
TWINS

1

—

Being stylish is more about
feeling good than it is
about looking good

1. The Non-Identical Twins

GENT NEXT DOOR

After spending my entire adult life designing, marketing, and styling fashionable clothes, I have written this book to reflect my thoughts, observations, and convictions on men's style. Clothing, fashion, and style are words so related that to define them can seem like trying to describe the colour grey. It can either be dark white or light black. Despite the close relations, the point is; grey is a colour by right, so is white, and so is black.

We do not need clothing to exist, just ask folks from indigenous tribes in parts of South America or Africa. They continue to live as thriving communities, yet wear little to no clothes. In the contemporary world we need clothes for health reasons, (staying warm, dry and clean) and to stay decent and out of jail (legal & social). This means clothing is a basic human need, but we are not basic creatures, are we? Neither are we content with having our 'basic' needs met. We are emotional, creative and ballistic creatures. Our need, desire, and uses for clothing reflect our nature, and here is where fashion and style enter the fray.

Style and fashion are like twins, they share the same DNA and metaphorically, the same parents. You could say that fashion and style are the offspring of clothes and human beings. Just as twins have their idiosyncrasies, fashion and style are non-identical twins. They are related, but their distinguishing features are clear. Style is *how* you wear your clothes, it is more of an attitude than a posture. Fashion is a construct driven by commerce and marketing. It is impossible to grasp what style is without relating to fashion, so let us try to define fashion, and perhaps, we will get a stronger vantage point on style.

Every September and February the world's media descend upon the major capitals of fashion, chiefly New York, London, Milan, and Paris. Designers of all pedigrees ranging from world-famous houses, such as Dolce & Gabbana, and Tommy Hilfiger to the brightest young artisans who have matriculated from fashion schools. Together they invest millions into runway shows and presentations. All in the name of capturing the imagination, column inches, social media feeds, and wallets of fashionistas, buyers, press, and influencers alike.

"Fashion is this vehicle of clothing painstakingly constructed then marketed like show business and fueled by our unquenchable thirst for newness."

To use an automotive metaphor, fashion trends arrive and thrive as quickly as a race car, then seem to fade away at equal velocity. Fashion, to survive, must continue to evoke a desire in us that needs to be satisfied immediately. Its relationship with our identity, culture, and sexuality means that this satisfaction is not forever but brief, perhaps six months at a time.

THE RISE OF MEN'S FASHION

If tradition is our yardstick, then fashion has predominantly been an industry catered to and consumed by women. The concept of *men's fashion* is a relatively fresh thing, while men's tailoring is steeped in tradition dating back centuries. Tailors are highly skilled specialists whose approach to design is more inclined to preserve tradition than drive innovation.

Historically, the changes in the way men dress have been slow and steady compared to women's fashion. This has now changed particularly since the turn of the millennium. Like an electric current, men's fashion now has market forces such as competition and consumer demands driving both innovation and reinterpretation of modes.

Between 2010 and 2015 the UK Menswear market grew by 22% and has outgrown the Womenswear market by 4% between 2015 and 2020.

This remarkable growth has been fuelled by Millennial males, who on average, spend £1, 276 a year on clothes. To put that into some context, men who are not Millennials spend an average of only £811 a year.

Men are now not only comfortable but anxious to show their personality and their creativity through what they wear. The rise of luxury streetwear and changing attitudes amongst men has ushered in a new generation of fearless and edgy menswear designers. Some of the most influential designers and brands include *Virgil Abloh (Off-White), Jerry Lorenzo (Fear of God), Kanye West (Yeezy), James Jebbia (Supreme), Brendon Babenzian (Noah) and Lev Tanju (Palace).*

Style is A Skill & A Tool

So fixated are human beings with personal appearance we fabricate it in all aspects of our lives. From employment and business, sports & entertainment, and perhaps most prominently in relationships. How we look is instrumental to how we feel, how we feel particularly about ourselves has a significant influence on how we perform in the key areas of our lives.

So considering this, I felt it right to share my persuasions that style is not just a novelty we read about, and aspire to have. Style is a learnable skill and a usable tool that we can exercise and develop. It extends our personality, our charm, and intrinsic value.

This book is a quick-fire road map on how to develop a personal style original to you, and how to use that style to attract what you want from life.

Whether it be for business success, career progression, attracting and keeping the woman you dream of, you are choosing the costume for these roles, every day. Here is your guide on how to choose well.

WHY IS
STYLE
RELEVANT?

—

2

"D I G N I T Y"
from Latin dignitas, from
dignus 'worthy'.
A composed or serious
manner or STYLE.

2. Why Is Style Relevant?

We have all heard the adage "never judge a book by its cover". The intentions behind this old mantra are noble, as it encourages us to look deeper, and not to superficial things. The problem is that our minds do not work like that, we judge things by their cover every day, and adversely, we are being judged based on our appearance too. Clothes communicate an impressive deal about you whether you are intentional about it or not because our brains can process visual details almost instantaneously.

Psychologists have coined this method of reading nonverbal cues as *Thin Slicing*. When we meet someone, we get a "gut feeling" about them. Instinctively, we may see them as being trustworthy, kind, or devious perhaps. All from a first impression that lasted around 30 seconds. We commonly refer to this "gut feeling" as intuition, and it is performed by our brain at a fast pace. Because of biological code passed through generations, and social conditioning, the human brain has learned to take a *'thin slice'* of the people we meet, and assess their personality.

Thin Slicing is how we subconsciously judge a book by its cover, even when we do not intend to. By understanding how clothing and dress impact people's thinking, we can curate what we wear into a personal style that helps influence the people around us. By developing personal style strategically, we can use it to advance our cause and enhance lives.

"What you wear and how you wear it is educating others about you by telling a story."

By understanding how clothing and dress impacts people's thinking, we can curate what we wear into a form of personal style that helps influence the people around us.

THE RESEARCH ON THIN slicing has concluded that our minds are surprisingly accurate at reading visual cues. So it is in our best interest to take an active and strategic approach to choose what clothes we wear and how we wear our clothes. Particularly in the crucial areas of our lives like work and business, in relationships, marriage, dating, and our fitness and wellness activities such as at the gym. The next time you are dressing up, consider the messaging you will emit while you are grooming, or perhaps fine-tuning your tie. Details like the way you tie your tie, can either say you are serious and articulate or you are casual and disorganised.

STYLE FOR
LOVE &
LIFE

—

3

3. Style For Love & Life

———

————————

'VISUAL IMPRESSIONS remain the most frequent pathway along which libidinal excitation is aroused' - Freud

With attraction, sex, and relationships, it is dangerous to make sweeping statements about gender behaviours. What we can say is that attraction is both biological and cultural, but where the boundary lines are on this dichotomy, is hard to locate. What is masculine and attractive in one part of the world, can be feminine in another cultural tradition. Men are attracted by what they see before they engage their other senses. While women are attracted by several things, perhaps most noticeably through the words they hear. If you think however that women do not notice pretty much everything you are wearing, then you are mistaken.

The Halo Effect

First impressions are judgments which occur within a few seconds of meeting someone. This is because of the brilliant ability of our brain to take a *'thin slice'* of a person's character and make a reasonably accurate assessment. The very first thing that makes an impression is the *halo effect*, this first impression then influences everything else you learn about someone.

Modern life in the digital age demands so much first impression management. Our image is marketing, from LinkedIn profiles and Instagram feeds, to online dating profiles. So we need to learn how to make these early assessments benefit us.

DATES & DATING SITES: *How to make Winning First Impressions*

Play to Your strength - If you are writing a blurb about yourself on a dating site, you want to start with your most positive characteristics. You only have one chance to make a first impression and you do not want your dating prospect to just swipe along. If you start with words like 'lazy' or 'untidy' and end with *'tall'* and *'funny'* the first two adjectives will have a greater influence on the dating prospect than the later. Given that *'lazy'* and *'untidy'* are typically unattractive traits, we would leave those to last or better yet, leave them out altogether.

From a styling point of view, you want to wear clothes that enhance your strengths, but stay true to who you are. This should apply for both a first date outfit and a profile photo. Strategic styling will become a powerful ally in your dating efforts, as it gives you the parameters to choose outfits that stay true to you.

Be Realistic - Make an honest assessment of the image you want to present. There are guys out there who have modest means, yet like wearing designer clothes on dates. The obvious rationale here is to impress the young lady with a perceived image of higher economic status. There is nothing wrong with this way of thinking if you are making it rain. But *don't be that guy* who lives vicariously through his Gucci loafers, most smart women can see through it, anyway. There's a difference between "dress to impress" and "flatter to deceive".

Avoid Assumed Similarity - On a first date, it may tempt you to anticipate what your date will wear. The temptation is then to try to match their assumed choice of outfit with yours. An example would be a guy who is pretty much always in a suit or blazer, is going on a date with a professional hockey player. He assumes that because she is a sporty girl, he will show up to the coffee date in his Adidas tracksuit with the inherent assumption that she will be in her sporting casuals too. *Don't be this guy*, stay true to your style archetype and be confident in it. A woman finds it attractive when a guy stands his ground and is confident in himself. Changing to impress her is a classic "nice guy" move and will only usher you closer to the dreaded friend zone. Besides, I was hired to style an Olympic Gold medalist, she was a female hockey star and there was a part of me that assumed she would be a frumpy, sporty dresser. Let me tell you. My jaw hit the floor. She was very elegant, so never assume.

Clothing Colour Can Affect Your Confidence with Women?

In the 1980s and 1990s, psychologists undertook extensive research to investigate the relationship between the colour of clothing and people's behaviour. Elliot & Maier developed Colour-in-Context theory, which found that when approaching a woman who you are romantically interested in, the colour of her clothes can evoke feelings of anxiety or confidence.

The authors also concluded that females are sensitive to colour cues in a social context and colour of clothing has an influence on their judgement of male attractiveness.

THE PSYCHOLOGISTS USED romance and achievement-based situations to determine if the colour red would make you more likely to approach or avoid a prospect. They used walking speed as their metric, as it is an established indicator of approach-avoidance motivation. The participants who took part in the test consisted of 64 Gettysburg College Undergraduates, 22 were male and 42 were female, with an average age of 18.95 years.

They assigned the participants to either a dating interview context or an intelligence interview context. Before the interviews with each participant, they were shown a headshot of the person who would interview them, the person in the headshot was of the opposite sex.

The individual in the pictures was wearing either a red t-shirt or a blue t-shirt. Straight after being shown the photos, the participants were told to walk down the hallway to a second room, where the interview would take place. The distance between the first and second room was 21 metres. They timed the participants in seconds from room one to the other.

The results revealed that red increased the walking speed of participants heading to an interview for a romantic related context, but decreased walking speed for interviews for an achievement-related context.

The same woman, when wearing a red t-shirt, as compared to wearing blue, was judged to be more attractive and have greater sexual intent. This is likely because of social priming, we have associated red with passion, romance and sexuality across mythology, literature, and fashion.

So essentially, it is not the colour itself we find attractive; it is the association we subconsciously make about that colour within the context of romance.

You are more likely to feel confident about approaching a woman who is wearing a shade of red than you are a woman wearing blue.

Purely because of the associations we have established with colours throughout the years. Interestingly enough, it may have an adverse effect if the same woman wearing red was interviewing you for a job or an academic exam.

Red in the animal kingdom is symbolic of both danger and sexual receptivity. Amongst some primates, males' with red chests or testicles show dominance and re-productivity. The results of the research suggest there are biological parallels between the instincts of primates and our human behaviour. Another interesting reasoning is that by wearing red, you are likely to be perceived as more dominant and confident by women.

Colour Can Work on You and Work for You

In 2010, Roberts SC, Owen RC and Havlicek published another study. They took an interest in determining whether clothing colour affected the wearer or the perceiver?

They took ten male and ten female participants and took photos of each wearing t-shirts in six unique colours, (red, blue, green, yellow and white) in random order. They then presented the images to 30 raters, all from the opposite sex, who provided ratings of attractiveness for each image on a scale of 0-10.

They then did a similar second test using the same images, but withheld the clothing through a grey, white and black digital render. The authors hypothesised that if the colour of clothes only affected perceivers, then the results would be the same when a model is photographed in red and any other colour. *Since this did not happen, they concluded that colour affects both the wearer of the clothes and the perceiver.*

They associated red and also black with higher attractiveness as both colours scored similarly high ratings. The authors also concluded that women are sensitive to colour cues in a social context, and colour influences their judgement of men's attractiveness.

These are just two scientific experiments, and I am sure further research will continue on this subject. But there is plenty of reasonable intelligence and wisdom we can draw from the results. Colours are emotional, they appeal to our soul, come to think of it, one of my teenage

Get photographed, wearing red and upload it as your dating app avatar, then show up on your first date wearing black!

CRUSHES WAS JULIA ROBERTS. Perhaps her most iconic image (*in my head*) is a scene in 'Pretty Woman' when she showed up at the hotel lobby and left Richard Gere speechless. Do you remember what she was wearing? Of course, you do.... a red dress!

Fitness & Style

When you wear sporty clothing, you invariably become more active and are more likely to go to the gym and workout. We explored earlier how intuitive our minds are at picking up cues and hunches. Our brain can also take the symbolic meaning of a particular item of clothing and convert it into motivation.

There was a study by Northwestern researchers. They used lab coats to test the effect our clothes have on attention-related activities (such as exercise). They found that the subjects who were wearing lab coats had a significant increase in sustained attention compared to those who did not wear lab coats.

They ran another test where they described the coats as "doctor's coats" and this increased the

subject's attention further. This was in sharp contrast to how subjects who wore lab coats described as a "painter's coat" were performing. The research shows that alongside the symbolic meaning we wrap around the clothes we wear, the experience of wearing clothes affects how we feel.

Does wearing an Anthony Joshua branded gym vest help you get some extra sets in at the gym?

If you buy quality, branded activewear at a price, it gives you a positive psychological push to wear those clothes and go to the gym. Fitness brands such as Lululemon have taken the athleisure trend by storm, with many of the women who wear their clothes sighting a boost in motivation to workout on the belief that they will look good doing it. As an elite level performer would tell you, it is everyday marginal gains that they are looking for from their sporting gear. They know that looking for big wins from equipment is improbable and at worst impossible. But if their clothing can add just an extra percentage to their performance each day, then those incremental gains become home runs overtime.

If you look good in your gym gear, you will probably feel better about being at the gym. You will feel more powerful and confident about crushing your fitness goals. Buy what you believe, *you* look good in. That's the key.

"All the world's
a stage"

WILLIAM SHAKESPEARE

4. Style For Your Success

E arlier, we established how your style sends messages to the world around you, but equally important is the messaging your style is sending to you.

Dress Formally is 'Social Distancing'

Much like language, dressing formally can create a social distancing. For example, we address unfamiliar people in informal ways rather than on a first-name basis. We also use more abstract language when we want to be polite. *"Specifically, as formal clothing is associated with enhanced social distance, we propose that wearing formal clothing will enhance abstract cognitive processing,"* -Journal Social Psychological Science.

Formal or Casual Clothing

One experiment involved 54 students brought both formal clothing and casual clothing and asked to interchange the outfits during the experiment. The idea was to test their cognitive processing *(thinking, knowing and remembering things)* to see if they focus on bigger, broader ideas or the finer details. The results showed that the students in formal clothing focused more on global processing than local processing compared to the students wearing street clothes.

We must put everything into its proper context. It is just one study and a small sample size of students cannot legislate for all men around the world. However, it is an interesting observation that would explain why corporate companies such as Banking and Law favour formal clothing.

CLOTHING AND COMPANY Culture

In 2010, Investment Bank UBS famously went viral when they published a manual instructing its banking employees how to dress.

GENT NEXT DOOR

The 44-page document was in French and dictated right down to the most hilarious detail of how the firm expects its employees to adorn themselves. Some amusing highlights were:

"Jacket buttons should be closed. When seated, they must always be open."

"A flawless appearance can bring inner peace and a sense of security."

"The shoulders should have natural proportions: if the shoulders are too broad you will appear too big with a too-small head."

"The jacket must completely cover your posterior." - Source UBS

I suppose what makes this such comedy gold is that it came from a global investment bank, not a fashion design house or a posh public school. Organisations in the more creative arena's have far more relaxed attitudes to workwear. Companies and Institutions like banks want to cultivate a culture and working atmosphere for abstract and concrete thinking and behaviours, creative organisations like Design Houses want to inspire abstract and more intuitive thinking.

This is all reflected in how the staff dress, showing that it is of no coincidence, how you dress does affect how you think, feel, and even perform in professional circles. Another word for a job is a role and like a stage actor playing a role, you should always dress for the part. As William Shakespeare put it *'All the World's A Stage'*

Another word for a job is 'role' and like a stage actor playing a role you should always dress for the part. As William Shakespeare put it 'All the World's A Stage'

Dressing For Interviews

What we need is a *"Horses for Courses"* approach as a successful interview outfit for one position may flop for another. Take some time and assess the context of the role and the company you are applying for. If you are a graduate applying for a Grad Scheme or junior position, then you should not show up looking like you are heading for the boardroom.

Wear a Suit; Men should as a first base, always look to wear a suit, but it must be a two-button suit. Three-button suits have not been in vogue since the 1990s, one-button suits are quite the opposite and are too fashionable *(unless it is a fashion position you are applying for).*

Wear a White Shirt; For a first interview, I would recommend you wear a white shirt. White is the colour of simplicity and suggests you are well-organised and trustworthy.

Wear A Watch (always); If you are serious about your career, then you will be serious about your time. It does not have to be a fancy watch, but you must wear one. It says that you value your time; you have goals, and you are ambitious.

Grooming; Leave no grey areas, if you are clean-shaven then be clean, if you are bearded then have a full well-groomed beard. Don't be somewhere in between. Ensure that your hair is clean, brushed, or combed.

Scent; Avoid wearing excessive amounts of cologne, there is nothing more annoying than when an overpowering smell will not leave a room, despite the absence of the person who brought it in.

#Tip *"Your Clothes Should Not Be Remembered" if they noticed your outfit then chances are it was not for a good reason. Occasionally this is the opposite, but only very occasionally.*

Styling for Casual Work & Business

The information age ushered in a new and somewhat infamous generation of tech-savvy, social and environmentally conscious knowledge workers. The buzz word from the post-1984 babies is Millennial. The generation which I am part of want bean bags and filtered coffee machines at work, we want flexible hours and if we are creatives, we would much rather work as home-based freelancers than traditional desktop employees.

Getting 'Smart Casual' right

This fresh attitude towards work has ushered in a more casual approach to business attire, particularly in industries that require a top level of intuitive and creative skills. Smart Casual is perhaps the hardest look to pull off for men because it is essentially an attempt to take two opposites and make them work in tandem. Now and again I enjoy going to a salsa night and when dancing with a partner for it to work, one has to lead (usually the man) and one has to follow (female partner). Smart casual is a bit of a dance, and like salsa one of these two powerful forces has to lead. Either you lead with smart and then 'casual' it down, or you start casual and 'smart' the lookup.

There are some foundational principles you can lean on to build a wardrobe of sound pieces that will go with almost anything else in your work wardrobe for most of the year.

Blazers & Unstructured Jackets

One of the biggest sartorial mistakes men make is wearing a suit jacket over some jeans or chinos searching for a classic smart casual look. The root cause of this is simple ignorance.

You must understand the difference between a blazer, sports jacket and a suit jacket.

A SUIT JACKET is paired with a matching pair of trousers made with fabric from the same roll. A Suit Jacket is tailored and finished in a very formal, clean way. When they are made and bought correctly, they fit really well. Please do not wear them over your jeans, you must wear a suit jacket as part of a suit.

A Blazer

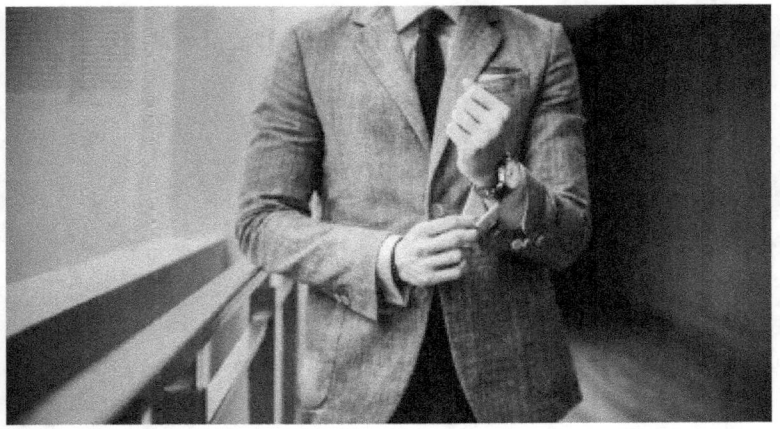

The Blazer is a bit of a hybrid; it is more formal than a sports jacket but made with similar principles to a suit jacket, just not with matching trousers. It will often have more subtle structuring to the shoulders, particularly in European trim, patch pockets, and the buttons stand out. Blazers will also likely come in lighter materials and are designed for formal lifestyle occasions like sports events.

Sports   *Jacket*

A Sports Jacket was originally designed for the sporting or active man to go recreational hunting. The jacket will have more profound pleats to encourage movement, elbow pads, a ticket pocket and a sports lapel are some typical hallmarks of a sports jacket. I would advise having a well made, well fitted woven wool blazer in a neutral colour for winter. I would then have a linen blend lightweight jacket in a spring colour. Cream for warm skin-undertones or sky blue or black for cool skin-undertones. *(See Chapter 7)*

This to avoid - *profound shoulder pads, you want to give off that relaxed vibe for business, squared shoulders can look too serious and stiff.*

Denim for Work

Now ripped jeans have been an absolute sales superstar in recent years, flying off the shelves from Primark to Prada. So it is likely that many of my readers are fans of ripped jeans. Perhaps you may work in a clothes shop or a fashion company, and the image culture in your workspace is to be fashion-forward, I would say ripped jeans is a go in this scenario. However, if you work in a setting that is slightly more corporate or perhaps you are a senior executive, I would encourage a choice of jeans that are equally fashionable but more conservative. You cannot beat a clean pair of well-fitting, high-quality dark navy or black jeans.

CASUAL SHIRTS

One way you can take smart items and make it casual is through versatile shirts such as Oxford shirts. They can come in shades of white, salmon pink, and

Light blue. They look sharp and relaxed, whether tucked or untucked while also keeping enough structure to be formal. Another great way to 'dress down' a formal look is through the collar design. The Chinese collar looks great inside a jacket or the shirt alone, particularly in linen material. You can also roll up the sleeves of your shirt, which is great for adding casual masculine elegance to a look.

Footwear

The suit with the trainer's look has become ever more prevalent and now makes appearances on celebrities at formal events. It does work well, so jump on board with this trend, however, ensure that the suit you're wearing is de-structured and not too finely tailored. I would also advise on keeping the trainers simple and in a single colour, flat sole trainers always look nice paired with a suit too.

Fabrics & Colours

Like colour, fabrics can be emotional, they change how an item feels on you but also how it makes others feel around you. Darker colours are dressier, and more formal, while brighter, lighter colours are more relaxed.

A linen suit immediately makes you 'casual' compared to traditional cotton or wool blend suits.

Fabrics for casual summer looks can include; *linen, silk and jersey*. Great casual fabrics for the winter months include *corduroy, suede, and mohair*.

Styling for Formal Work & Business

Suiting

For all you gentlemen out there who wear a smart suit and tie to work every day. I would recommend building a collection of 3 to 6 suits split equally for each season.

Suit Colours

Navy Blue and Charcoal grey should be your foundation. Add a Black suit for dressier work-related activities, like formal parties, dinners, or award ceremonies.

Lapels

As a base, your first three suits should be notch lapels which are classical and simple. Your dressier black suit can be in peak lapels as they are more of a statement of intent, peak lapels are also good for the boardroom.

Breast & Buttons

The single-breasted two-buttoned suit has been the go-to workwear for over ten years now. It flatters the figure and can make you appear taller. A one buttoned suit is great if you are taking a client out for a semi-casual lunch or you have a press day to host as they are slightly more fashionable and approachable. Once you have a foundation of 3 suits in your wardrobe, you can add a double-breasted option. The double-breasted suit has made a real resurgence and can work for ultra-formal business meetings and at weddings and funerals because of its military references.

Double-breasted with 6 buttons

Single-breasted with 2 buttons

DOUBLE-BREASTED VS Single-Breasted

FIT & CUT

You want a fit that is as close to a tailored-fit as possible. I would not advocate a skinny suit for work, you would not want to show up for business looking like an Avenger. An oversized suit just looks lazy so find a suitable fit somewhere in-between. There is one big *must*; the shoulders must fit well, shoulder overhang is simply unacceptable.

Shirts

Much like the suit itself, you want to get as close to a well-tailored shirt as you can. There are two things you *must* avoid. *'Pirate Sleeves'* which are a combination of baggy arms with well-cinched cuffs, even if you have skinny arms you can still find a cut that does not leave all that excess fabric. The other thing you must avoid is *"Flying Squirrels"* which is when you have excess fabric under the arm-pits. This looks particularly bad when you wear a waistcoat. In terms of colours, white is a superb choice if you are pitching an idea to superiors, or potential clients. I would recommend 8 - 12 shirts, at least a third of them must be a variation of white.

Accessories

A **pocket square** is great for adding colour to your look but wear a different colour tie. You do not want to look like you are wearing last year's box-set Christmas present from TK Maxx. **Cufflinks** are an opportunity to show your personality so go for something cheeky that a potential client or partner may ask you about at networking drinks. During the winter, you can wear whacky brightly colour socks and when the weather improves, you can even opt to wear penny loafers with exposed ankles. Always be mindful of your audience though, going sockless may not work when you are presenting to directors.

Timepiece for Work

One of the more sensible stipulations from the UBS 'how to dress' manifesto was *"If you wear a watch, it suggests reliability and that punctuality is of great concern to you"*

Your watch game will have to be on point, particularly if you work in the financial sector. Not everyone can afford a Rolex or an Omega, and that is fine. I would recommend sticking to traditional watchmakers, rather than buying a Michael Kors or other designer names you find in the local, or online catalogue.

Shoes

Your shoes are like the back cover of a book, this is when you sell yourself or sell yourself short. You may recall the famous scene in Kingsman's quote *"Oxford not Brogues"* I would always advise that every man should invest in a top-quality pair of Oxfords. Oxfords are iconic and timeless and are still *the* quintessential choice for true below the knee style. Closed lacing distinguishes Oxford's from the similar-looking Derby's, they were made popular by renegade students at Oxford University in the 19th century and have never looked back since.

You may also prefer brogues which are another classical shoe style for business and perhaps this is where the argument and some confusion come. You can find Oxford shoes that look like brogues and brogues that look like Oxfords. Brogues get their

name from the leather ornamentation known as broguing with carved holes in the leather. Back in the 19th-century men would wear these shoes through wetlands and the holes would allow water to drain out once back on dry land. The active and recreational roots of Brogues are why they are a more casual choice as compared to Oxfords, which are strictly business. Monk Strap and Penny loafers are timeless options which would not look out of place at Bank tube station either.

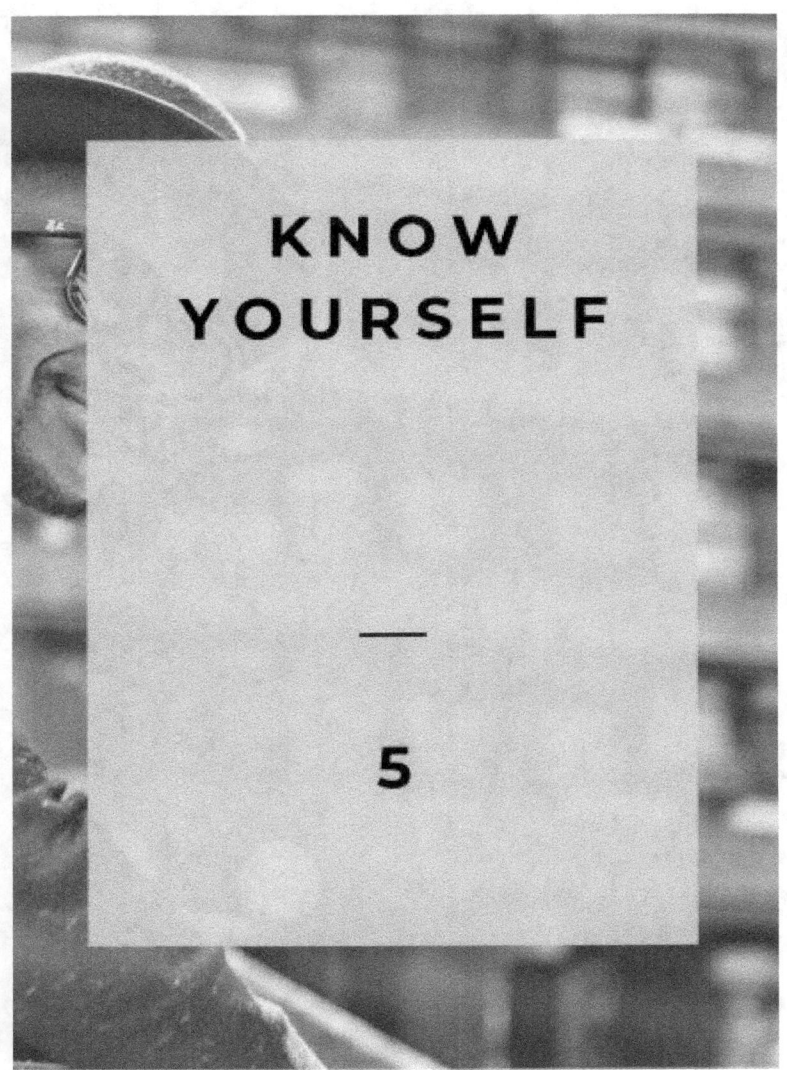

KNOW YOURSELF

—

5

"Style is the image of character"

EDWARD GIBBON

5. Know Yourself

A sk yourself a question.

When I meet people, what impression do I want to leave on them?

The first thing you can do is take an inventory of your body. Now, I know guys can feel too macho and important to look at their body shape. Little do you know that the selective ignorance of your body structure could be why you wear the wrong suit for your build and maybe the reason you have not received a promotion at work.

We all at various stages of our lives wish we were taller, or wealthier, or better looking. I am reminded of my insecurities during my teen years, although I was a talented athlete and popular with the girls, I was always skinny, which affected my confidence a bit. At 23 I had to learn to accept my skinny legs, I would not develop thighs like Jack Wilshere, nor was I going to make it to 6 foot.

Thankfully, as I have matured, I have shaken off my insecurities and in my late twenties, my legs filled up. I now have something that slightly resembles calf muscles. Yey!

2 Things to Remember:

Dressing well is about *BALANCING* SHAPES and managing the proportions of our body, so they look even.

Then, it is about *BALANCING COLOURS*, by wearing shades that complement your skin, so you stand out and look your best.

How I know Myself

I have learned to make the most of my slim, athletic frame. I will break down each component of dressing well in the coming chapters, but as a template, below I summarize how I apply each component to my style.

BODY TYPE: Wedge Shaped

1. I have short legs so I wear slim-fitting trousers. They define the silhouette, giving the illusion of my legs being longer.

2. My shoulders are athletic, but my chest measures just 37 inches. To find balance, a biker jacket with imposed shoulder padding broadens my shoulders. By having a narrow waist (30 inches), I make the most of this feature through well-fitted clothes, giving me the desirable 'V' torso shape. I want to show this off because a wedge-shaped chest is a sign of masculinity and strength to females.

3. My long skinny neck means I avoid wearing v-necks as they make my neck appear even longer. Turtle-necks, however, are a treat in the winter, and a simple crew-neck (round shape) works in the warmer months.

Skin Undertone: Neutral

A neutral skin undertone means I can wear most colours and make them work. We will go into greater depth on how you can find your skin undertone, and what colours will work for you later.

Colours that compliment me: Black, white, red, beige, army green and mid blues.

Colour Pairing: By wearing darker trousers my legs will look slightly longer, a brighter top will focus the attention on my athletic torso which is my stronger feature.

Being shorter than average, vertical lines elongate my silhouette. I achieve these vertical illusions through pinstripe suits or narrow lapels.

Next, I will show how you can discover your body shape and your skin undertone, and how to use it to your advantage.

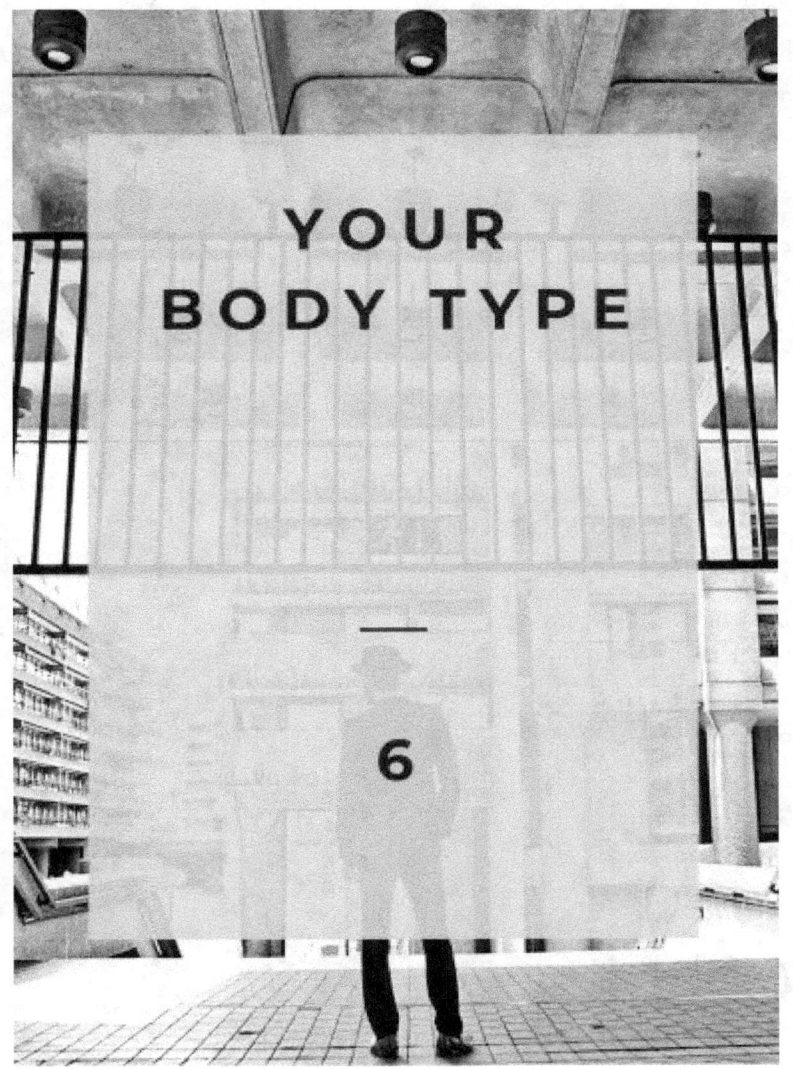

YOUR
BODY TYPE

—

6

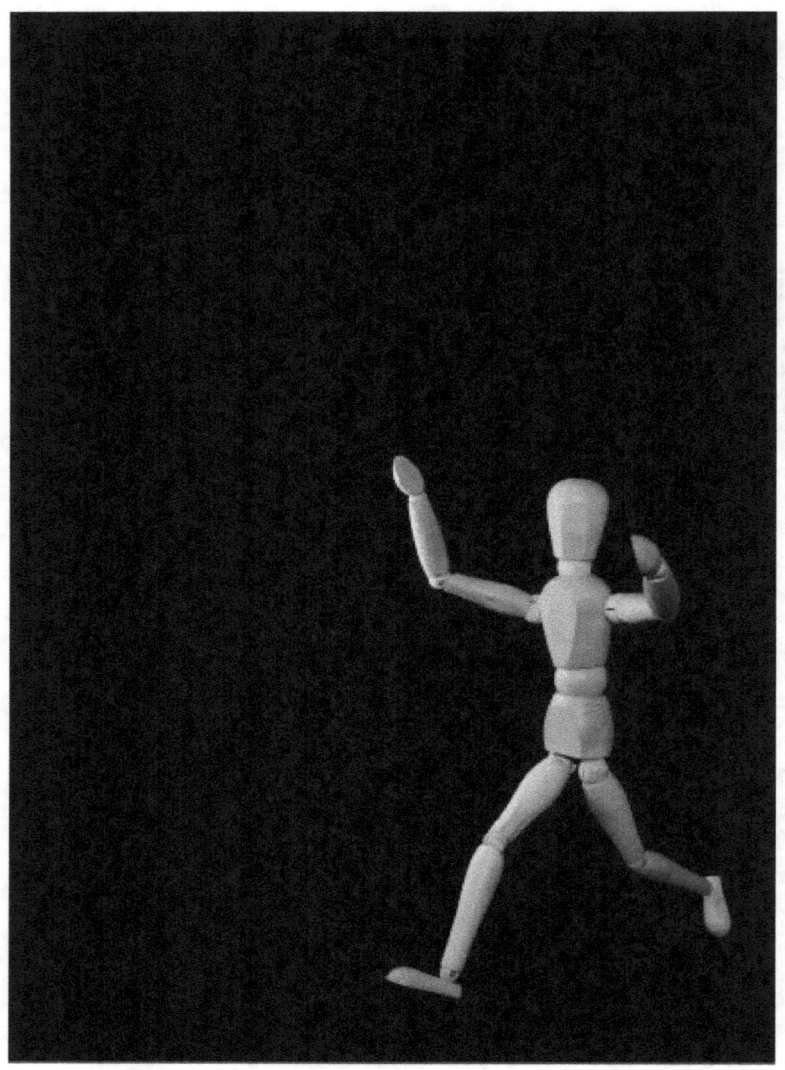

6. Your Body Type

———

Y ou see it all over women's lifestyle magazines and beauty blogs; *"5 perfect dresses for your body-shape"*, and so on. I will admit that taking an inventory of your body shape is not exactly the most stimulating activity for the male ego. But men need to take as much care as women in dressing according to the figure.

A few things to first consider

1: Dress for the body shape you have today, not the body you aim to have tomorrow.

2: Seek the body shape that is most desirable in your culture. Not all cultures and ethnicities share the same body ideals. And thank goodness for that. I base this advice on a mostly western, masculine, body ideal. This is a well proportioned muscular silhouette with broad shoulders, narrow waist and full thighs and calves.

3. Sizes differ in each geographical region, a size medium in the United States will be bigger than a size medium in the UK, which will be bigger than a size medium in Japan.

Proportion is key. *This is rule number 1, so let me say it again. Proportion is key.*

The three fundamental body types for men

1. Inverted Triangle
2. Trapezoid
3. Rectangle

Most men's body shapes will fit in and around these three variants, regardless of weight and height.

Inverted Triangle or Wedge

INVERTED TRIANGLE OR Wedge

If you look into a full-length mirror and your chest and shoulders are wider than your hips, then you have an inverted triangle body shape.

You may spot extreme examples of this body shape in your local gym with guys who resemble Johnny Bravo. If you are wedge-shaped, it's nothing to worry about, apart from maybe two leg days per week until those pins fall into proportion a bit.

Things to Avoid

Top: Polo t-shirts or jumpers with horizontal stripes above the belly button are a no-go for you.

Why: *Horizontal Shapes broaden the upper part of your body and patterns will draw more attention to this area.*

Middle: Blazers & suit jackets with exaggerated shoulder pads.

Why: *They will draw more attention to your shoulders.*

Bottoms: Skinny Jeans

Why: *they will only accentuate your thin legs, giving you the shape of a doner kebab.*

Things to wear

Tops: V-neck t-shirts, and tops with stretchy fabrics that fit snug.

Why: *To elongate your upper torso and keep a nice tapered look around the waist. Caution, however, deep v-neck tops are uncool so keep it subtle.*

Middle: Pinstriped suits, striped shirts, sports jackets.

Why: *Vertical lines will help give the illusion of a narrow upper torso. Relaxed tailoring for your jackets and Blazers will make your shoulders less severe.*

Bottoms: Tapered Jeans, Cargo Chinos, Suede Boots, Chunky Trainers.

Why: *Straight jeans can look awkward and out-dated particularly for shorter guys, a tapered fit is a great compromise between skinny and straight fit. Cargo chinos will add size to your thighs, while boots and shoes with volume will draw attention to your feet. This will help balance out the proportions of your silhouette.*

The Trapezoid

THE TRAPEZOID

Common consensus says the 'perfect body' for a woman is an hourglass, the notion being a balanced distribution of curves either side of a slim waist and flat stomach. I am not a believer of 'ideal' body types, I subscribe to the old saying of "different strokes" et al. If you have athletic broad shoulders and chest, and an even distribution of muscle down your waist and legs then you have the consensus choice for the 'perfect body'.

Things to avoid

Tops: Regular fit shirts, Tight t-shirts, Scoop neck tops.

Why: *Volume has made a return and over-sized is a thing, but a regular fit shirt with an excessive overhang at the waist when tucked in, is unforgivable. Scoop neck t-shirts can extend the width of your shoulders which can of-set the balance of your silhouette. Guys with muscular physiques can easily overcompensate and wear skin-tight t-shirts. Women find this a turnoff, they can already see you have an impressive body, just leave enough room for the imagination*

Middle: Skinny fit suits

Why: *Not only are they becoming dated, but it suggests to the beholder you are trying too hard to show everyone you have muscles. It can be hard for muscular guys to get a suit right for them.*

Bottoms: *There are very few items you cannot wear because your body is so well proportioned. If you have big thighs avoid getting trousers with restrictive room up top, particularly during warmer months.*

Things to wear

Tops: Sportswear, V-neck t-shirts, Polo t-shirts, fine knit roll neck sweaters, Sports Jacket.

Why: Take advantage of the accessibility of your host shape with items that taper elegantly around your shoulders and cinched at the abs. This gives off the classic 'V' masculine shape. Sports Jacket is a smart option as they have less structured shoulder padding.

Middle: A Tailor, Slim fit trousers, Skinny Jeans

Why: If you are a huge guy like Dwayne Johnson, most off-the-peg suits in shops won't fit you. Find a tailor, or if it's beyond your wallet, go for a slim fit suit and have it altered by a local seamstress. Your suit jacket should have subtle shoulder padding as your physique already provides structure. Slim fit or cropped trousers would look awesome on you and so do skinny jeans.

Bottoms: Trainers, Casual Shoes, Sliders, Sandals

Why: Your natural shape has a lot of structure, relaxed footwear breaks up that structure and gives you a bit of fluidity. In the summer months showing your feet helps you, so go for sandals or sliders.

THE RECTANGLE OR SQUARE

If you find that you have more or less perfect alignment between your shoulders and your waist then you are a rectangle body shape. The key for you is to add structure by broadening the shoulders, then tapering the waist.

Things to avoid

Tops: t-shirts or sweaters with vertical lines, longline t-shirts or shirts.

Why: *The more vertical lines the more the illusion of a square the perceiver will see. Longline tops suggest to the eyes to look down and we want to look across, particularly at the upper chest and shoulders.*

Middle: Double-breasted Suit, unstructured jackets, Bomber Jacket

Why: *Double Breasted Jackets or Suit will emphasise the rectangular shape and may look like it is being worn on a hanger, not a person. Avoid anything without structure to it, so a jacket like bombers with no shoulder padding is not a good idea.*

Bottom: Baggy jeans, Baggy sweatpants

Why: *Anything without any structure is not going to work for you, so loose-fitting trousers or sports bottoms will drape down like a curtain if you are tall and will balloon around if you are shorter.*

Things to Acquire

Tops: Shirts with shoulder straps, patterns and bright colours, polo t-shirts, army jumpers.

Why: *Bright colours, prints, padding or straps along the shoulders, upper chest, and neck will draw attention towards those areas to give a broader structure against your waist.*

Middle: Single-breasted blazer & Suit Jacket, Biker Jacket, Trench Coat.

Why: *Jackets with a structure to the shoulders will give them a broader and more pronounced illusion. On a single-breasted jacket, the V line sloping towards your waist will give you a lovely wedged shape.*

BOTTOM: Regular chinos, straight cut/ tapered jeans.

Why: *Tailored trousers add structure with a hint of shape to your legs, giving you a balanced proportion.*

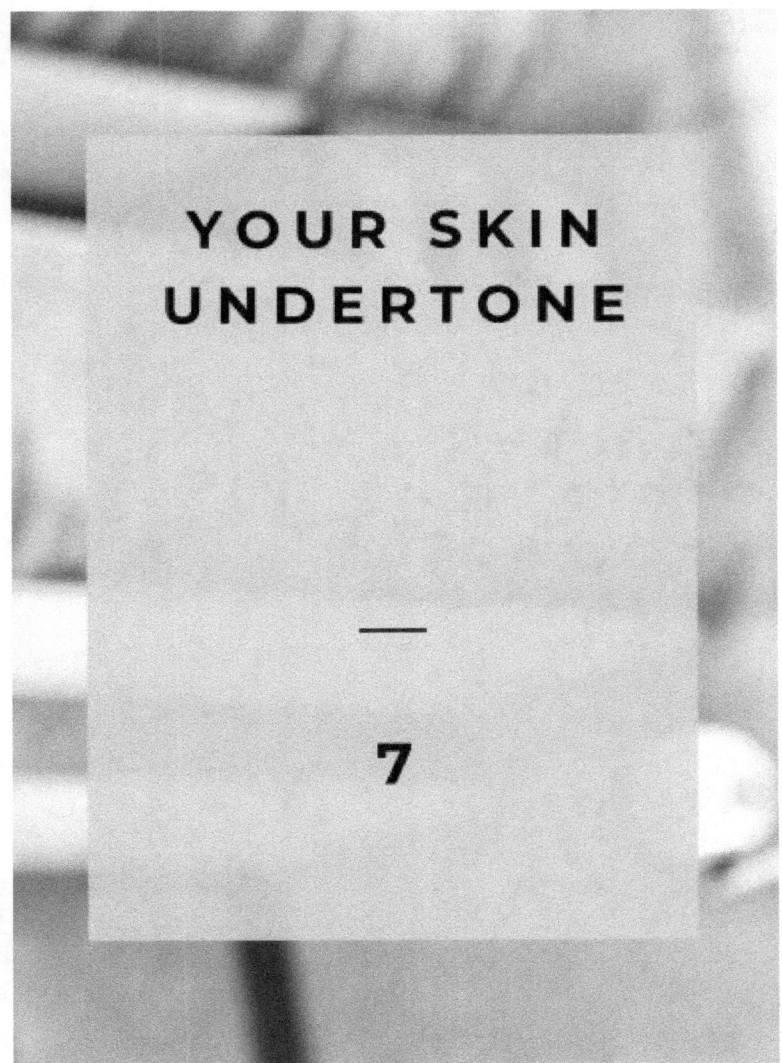

YOUR SKIN UNDERTONE

—

7

One can speak
poetry just by
arranging
colours well

VINCENT VAN GOGH

7. Your Skin Undertone

S o we have talked about your body type as that is the actual tool that your clothes will fit on. Now we will look at another crucial area of style, colours. You may find something they like and choose it in your favourite colour without considering whether that colour looks any good on you.

Now I will preface this by saying; what I will share with you here is a guideline, a yardstick you can use to help you look and feel your best as a man. We have centred much of traditional colour theory around the colour wheel, using it as a tool to find colours that match and complement one another. I appreciate the colour wheel and believe there is a place for it in fashion design. However, in styling and personal style specifically, it is a waste of time. Colours are emotional things, they evoke certain attitudes, feelings, and even values both for the wearer and the beholder. Let us explore the basic inherent characteristics associated with some common colours.

Colours are Emotional & Have Meaning.

Red is very provocative, it represents passion, desire, danger and alarm. It is the colour you wear to show boldness, no one is trying to blend in when they are wearing red. (unless you are an Arsenal fan). This is not the colour to wear for more conservative occasions like funerals or a court appearance.

Blue has an impressive breadth to its uses. Navy blue represents security and professionalism, think banks or law firms so navy should be your first port of call for a job interview outfit. Mid Blues are sad and can express feelings of loneliness or sorrow. Think of the origins of 'Blues' music or the term 'feeling blue'. Light Blues are on the other side of the spectrum and make us feel comforted and safe. Light blues are the colour of caregiver organisations such as charities and health organisations. Light blues are brilliant choices for summer dating outfits and leisure activities.

Green represents newness or freshness; we understand it to be the colour most kind for the eyes to rest on. Green is the colour of nature and has therapeutic qualities that help relieve stress, hence why people like to go for walks in and around nature to declutter.

Regardless of your race or complexion, skin tone either has a warm undertone or a cool undertone.

You can be white and have a warm undertone and you can be black and have a cool undertone. Some people have quite a neutral undertone to their skin. Neutral undertones can wear pretty much any colour and their skin will pop.

TINASHE DENNIS IMMANUEL

HOW TO DISCOVER YOUR Skin Undertone.

Below are easy practical hacks you can use to find out what skin undertone you have.

#Hack 1 Wrist Veins

If you survey the veins on your wrist carefully under clear daylight and the shade of your veins are a more green colour as opposed to blue then you have a warm skin undertone. Adversely if your veins are bluer, then you have a cool skin undertone. If your veins are like mine and flush compared to your skin tone, then you are somewhere in the middle (neutral).

#Hack 2 Gold & Silver Jewelry

If you get a hold of a piece of gold jewellery and silver jewellery, it could be a watch, bracelet, or your partner's earnings and just compare it against your skin. If you find that the silver jewellery complements your skin better than the gold then you have a cool undertone, if the gold works better for you then you have a warm undertone. If both seem to work well, then you are somewhere in the middle.

Red with Blue undertones, Pastel Colours (particularly if you are blonde), Neons, Greyscale, Winter whites.

COLOURS FOR WARM SKIN UNDERTONES

Red with orange undertones, Black (looks fantastic with warm skin tones), Purple, Olive Green, Earth tones, Bold Colours, Yellow.

PASTEL SHADES, MILD yellows, Sapphire Blue, Black

In the United Kingdom, where I live, the most commonly worn colour by men is black followed closely by dark blue and grey. This is a cultural thing mainly driven by our rather drab climate. However, I would like to challenge men to not leave women to have all the fun with adding colour to your wardrobe, even if you are reading this and you live in Western Europe or a cold climate. I would encourage you to give the jewellery and vein hacks a go, then try out some colours suggested in your local menswear store. It would excite me to receive your feedback on your experience.

YOUR STYLE ARCHETYPE

—

8

" style is a way of
saying who you are
without having to
speak"

RACHAEL ZOE

8. Your Style Archetype

What is an Archetype

An archetype can be known as a universal symbol or character. We base much of the intellectual commentary of archetypes on Carl Jung's work. Jung was a Swiss psychologist credited with coining the introvert and extrovert personalities theory. He also coined the term "collective unconscious" which refers to experiences shared by a social group, such as love, religion, death, struggle, and survival. He propounded that we recreate these experiences in literary works and art in the form of characters, story plots or general themes. So, for example, we see the hero archetype portrayed prominently in cinema, from Superman and Captain America to James Bond and Jason Bourne.

Archetypes are Not Stereotypes

It is also important to clarify that an archetype is not a stereotype, archetypes focus on function as opposed to superficial details. An archetype depicts an individual's role; it does not define personality or depth. An example could be a *Stereotype* of a Physics Professor, could be a middle-aged or older white man with grey hair and a poorly kept beard but an *archetypical* Physics professor could be a woman of Asian descent who plays recreational rugby and lifts weights.

Your Style Archetype

Your body type and skin tone are about styling our external person, your archetype simplifies styling to express your personality and mission.

GND'S 7 STYLE ARCHETYPES

What we can extrapolate from Jung's work is that archetypes are universal symbols that evoke specific characteristics that influence the audience's perception both unconsciously and emotionally. This makes them very useful tools in non-verbal forms of communication such as personal style.

When your purpose and archetype become congruent with your style, you will become an attractive force to potential suitors, socially, professionally and romantically.

Here 7 Archetypes which encapsulate personalities, colours, attitudes and values. Included are examples of famous men who evoke these archetypes through a combination of their purpose, public image, and distinct sense of style.

1. **The Classic Man**

Motivation: *To lead and inspire others and command respect.*

The Classic Man

Example: David Beckham

In his playing days, he ushered in the era of the metrosexual man, as he has gotten older Beckham has become a bastion for so many good causes. Most prominently is his work as a UNICEF Ambassador. Gone are the blonde highlights Beckham dresses in imperiously tailored suits or classic biker jackets.

This is Your Style Archetype if: you live much of your life around formal settings and are a man on a mission with serious responsibilities. You enjoy and value sartorial traditions and do not fuss about trends. You may have a tailor or perhaps aspire to have one, then once you do, everything will come full circle. Finally, you will find that elusive, perfect suit.

Brands to follow: *Ermenegildo Zegna, Huntsman, Hugo Boss, Giorgio Armani, Calvin Klein, Canali, TM Lewin.*

---

2. The Melodramatic Man

TINASHE DENNIS IMMANUEL

MOTIVATION: Self-expression, rather than fitting-in

The Melodramatic Man

Example: Kanye West

Kanye is a classic creator, he always seems restless to see a vision come to fruition. Whether it is music or fashion, Kanye always has a desire to do what no one else is doing. He mixes cosy sweaters with futuristic jeans, and footwear, nothing is conventional about his style. He is not into tradition or timeless style; he is all about innovative fashion.

This is Your Style Archetype if: you are borderline avant-garde with your fashion taste but also like things to be comfortable and sporty. You hate fitting in so you are happy to spend on luxury, you want to find new edgy designer's that *'no one knows about'* so you raid luxury boutiques like Dover Street Market.

Brands to follow: *Commes Des Garçon, Y-3, Yeezy, Kenzo, Fear Of God, Vetemens.*

---

3. The Utility Man

MOTIVATION: Independence and a sense of adventure.

The Utility Man

Example: Bear Grylls

Can a man who self-isolated himself in a remote forest show us anything about style? Away from the field, Bear is an impressive example of how to rock the roll-up sleeves look. Bear's clothing is casual, with natural earth tones, easy knitwear, and rugged boots.

This is Your Style Archetype if: you are the guy who wants to find pieces that work well without thinking too much about it each morning. This is the archetype for hard-working men, who are lazy about fashion. You are happy to spend but you want quality; you want clothes that will last you years, so contemporary menswear and workwear styles are your refuge.

Brands to follow *Barbour, Red Wing, Timberland, Hiut Denim, Edwin, A.P.C., Universal Works, Dickies.*

———————————

1. The Romantic Man

MOTIVATION: *Charming and sensitive, the romantic man reflects this by his love for luxury.*

The Romantic Man

Example: Ryan Gosling

We know Ryan Gosling for his bold suits on the red carpet, whether it is an old Hollywood inspired ivory dinner jacket or a textured brown suit. Gosling nails casual too. A famous look was a nautical-inspired Ralph Lauren polo he wore at Cannes. Gosling always looks like the guy you would like your daughter to marry.

This is Your Style Archetype if: you are what they call a 'purist'. You have wonderful knowledge and interest in fashion, and you thrive to take tradition and add modern flair to it. You do not just wear your clothes, you study them, you know the stories about the designers. If you are the guy who reads GQ, attends Men's Fashion Week or Pitti Oumo, then this is the archetype for you.

Brands to follow *Paul Smith, Dolce & Gabbana, Gucci, Lanvin, Ozwald Boateng, Reiss, Fendi.*

———

5. The Impish Man

MOTIVATION: *Rebellious, but humorous. He wants to bend the rules.*

The Impish Man

Example: Russell Brand

GENT NEXT DOOR

Russell Brand seems to be able to chameleon his way into people's minds via laughter. He wants to look like it took not much thought in choosing his clothes, yet somehow it works. In his younger days, his style was very much a Pete Doherty-Esque Camden grunge rocker, but he has evolved somewhat since. His clothing is never dull, always accessorised and theatrically styled, like having half his shirt unbuttoned.

This is Your Style Archetype if: you like your heavy metal rock music, or prefer to be in goth black all the time. If you enjoy motorcycling in leathers and live life to the full, then this is the archetype for you. Signature styles will include ripped jeans, black denim, military print, and short leather biker jackets.

Brands to follow: *Vivienne Westwood, Alexander McQueen, Balmain, All Saints.*

6.   THE   BOYISH   MAN

THE BOYISH MAN

Motivation: *This is the man who fosters an attitude of playfulness and boyish cheek.*

Example: Pharrell Williams

The ageless Pharrell is the greatest music producer of his generation, but he is a fashion icon too. Whether he is wearing a vintage workwear-inspired double denim outfit or a tailcoat tuxedo, Pharrell's style keeps a sense of humour about it. He always seems to have fun with what he is wearing, he is the Peter-Pan of fashion.

This Is Your Style Archetype if: you were the guy that wore your school uniform immaculately but experimented with your tie length. Preppy style fits into the Boyish archetype, as it suggests a relaxed sophistication. If you like colour, prints, bow-ties and clear geeky glasses then this is the archetype for you.

Brands to follow: *Tommy Hilfiger, Ralph Lauren, Lacoste, Burberry, Aquascutum, Fred Perry, Brooks Brothers.*

7. The Drip Man

Motivation: *Work hard, play hard, and spend big. This guy follows trends, but not high street trends, only the most gangsta trends will do.*

The Drip Man

Example: A$AP Rocky

A$AP is a hybrid, he can look hood rich Harlem by day, then show up in Manhattan at night, dripping in Dior. He does it with all the swag and badassery that Harlem is renowned for.

This is Your Style Archetype if: you are heavy into your hip-hop and urban culture. You do not have to be black; you do not have to be from an urban community, and you do not have to be young. This expression of fashion is about relevance, comfort and being part of a movement that wears snapbacks, skater hats, and beats headphones. You need to stay in touch with the latest releases in rap music, sneakers, and designer collaborations.

Brands to follow Supreme, HBA, Palace, Bape, Stussy, Stone Island, Off-White, Jordan's.

HOW TO IDENTIFY YOUR Style Archetype

Now I will preface this by saying that each of us probably evokes a combination of two or three archetypes in the unique roles we have in life. For example, as a father, you may be the hero to your children, the caregiver to your wife and at work, you are the office joker. What we want to focus on is distinguishing your archetype(s) that is synonymous with your purpose and authentic to your personality.

1: *Pick two style archetypes which attract you to the most. The first will be your primary and then a secondary archetype that you most like to evoke aesthetically.*

2: *Then speak to the five people closest to you. It could be a spouse, parent, sibling or colleague, as long as they know you very well. Now, without* *revealing the archetypes you chose, ask them to describe your style in five words.*

What we are trying to do, is to find a commonality between the archetype which attracts you and the archetype you naturally evoke to the key people around you.

If you do not narrow down your focus to what authentically aligns to your character then you are very vulnerable to simply being a victim of the fashion machine and looking like everybody else.

Your Archetype is Your Personal Brand Image

People who know you well will recognise the archetype you evoke because your behaviour and appearance will consistently evoke it. This right here is your brand image. If there are several archetypes chosen by your friends, then do not be anxious. Earlier, we established that we naturally evoke a few archetypes, depending on our roles, and the environments we spent our lives in.

How to use your archetype

So we have identified your archetype now we want to explore how to create your style archetype. Certain types of clothing evoke certain ideas, attitudes, and perhaps even values, we want to be aware of this when composing a wardrobe synonymous with your archetype. If you want to be a classic gentleman, then you want to pick out clothing which is very much sartorial in style. Consult a tailor and get some advice on what types of suits would suit you best; we will explore this further later.

Knowing and understanding your style archetype will give you clarity and focus. The modern world is competitive and homogenous. If You do not narrow down your style to what authentically aligns to your character, then you are very vulnerable to being a victim of the fashion machine and looking like everybody else. From a micro perspective, by applying the filter of the archetype, you know exactly what you want from the world and you can show up looking your best authentic self.

The human mind naturally tries to put everything into categories, when you get good at dressing as your primary and secondary archetype, The minds of your business contemporaries, clients, potential love interests, spouse or girlfriend are put at ease. We cut their journey of understanding what you stand for short. They can now interpret the role you will play in their life much sooner than the next guy. We also know this is also as *having an edge.*

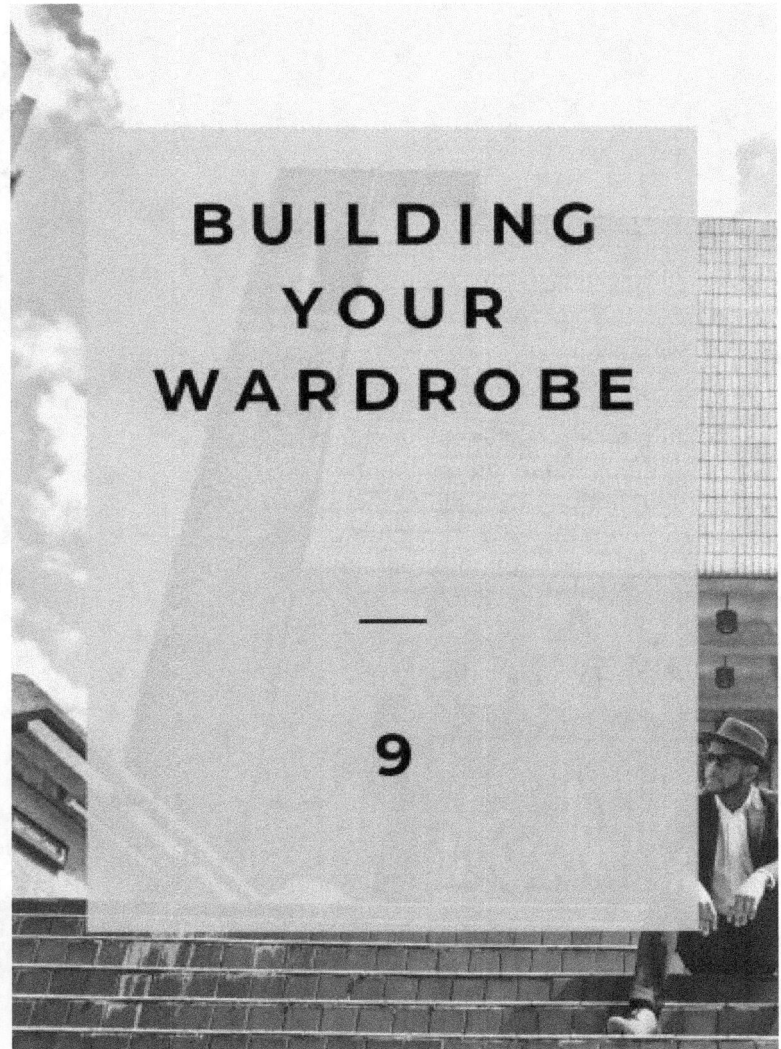

BUILDING
YOUR
WARDROBE

—

9

"Whether we're talking socks or stocks, I like buying quality merchandise when the market is down."

WARREN BUFFETT

9. Building Your Wardrobe

The Buffet Effect

I recall a shopping trip with two of my friends; it was a few days after New Year' 2003. The January sales were on, I had just got paid so my friends and I hopped on the Tube down to Oxford Street. We spent two hours visiting all the popular high street shops, then checked out the flagship Levi's store, which at the time was on Regent Street. As I browsed through the denim and outerwear my eyes rested upon a stunning distressed black denim jacket. It had a sheep-fur style lining with the fir continuing to the collar and sleeves.

It was love at first sight, I immediately pulled it off the railing to try it on. At the back of my mind, I was crushed because I knew I couldn't afford it. The jacket sat on my skinny frame wonderfully. It had a nice tailored cut and fitted snug on me. Wearing that jacket my shoulders and arms immediately felt more muscular, and I just loved the fur collar. I stepped out of the changing rooms to get a second opinion from my friends. *"Oh, my days Bruv that looks sick on you!"* That was the reaction from my best friend John.

The sales assistant then told me the jacket came with matching jeans. The suit besotted me, but I had a heavy heart because it was way beyond my budget, at least that's what I thought. My friend Blanchard encouraged me to buy it and reminded me that since it's January, I should check to see if it is on sale. I checked the price tag and 'oh snap!' it was actually for sale. Both the jeans and jacket had a 40% discount. Here I am years later, as I write this chapter, that denim jacket is still an integral part of my wardrobe. I discovered that day the value of investing in quality clothes that are not trend-driven but timeless pieces with an intrinsic value to them. When I wear my Levi's jacket, it looks like a vintage denim jacket. I haven't put on an impressive deal of weight since my late teens (thankfully) so I fit in the jacket even better now. I paid around 160.00 GBP for both the jeans and jacket. I owned it for twelve years without the need to discard or replace it.

"Price is what you pay, value is what you get."

WARREN BUFFETT

This is when this story links with the Warren Buffet quote above. The world's greatest investor has built a fortune that even King Solomon would be proud of through buying shares in dominant companies. *The Oracle of Omaha* has become famous for mastering the art of buying   great   stocks   when   they   are   *'on   sale'.*

"Our favourite holding period is forever."

WARREN BUFFETT

By buying clothes less often in smaller quantities you give yourself room to set aside some capital for those significant opportunities when an item becomes available at a discount. You then build a foundation of high-quality wardrobe staples which will last you a long time. Making investments is crucial for success in life, that goes for finances, relationships, and personal style. Therefore, have the discipline to buy luxury when you can. The quality and craftsmanship will ensure that it lasts a long time and will always remain stylish. Warren Buffett is as famous for not selling his shares as he is for buying great stocks. Hence why the quote: *'our favourite holding period is forever!'* Once Buffett buys a stock, he never really intends to sell it as long as he feels it is a high-quality company.

Market forces impel both the stock market and fashion trends. Buffett's investment philosophy does not take a liking to market trends and the day to day 'trading' that happens on Wall Street or the City of London. Instead, he likes to keep things simple. Buffet wants to buy excellent companies who he believes are selling at a price lower than their intrinsic value, hence why they are *on sale*. We can extrapolate principles from Warren Buffett's financial investing to our wardrobe building. Instead of stocks, we are investing in great *timeless* clothes.

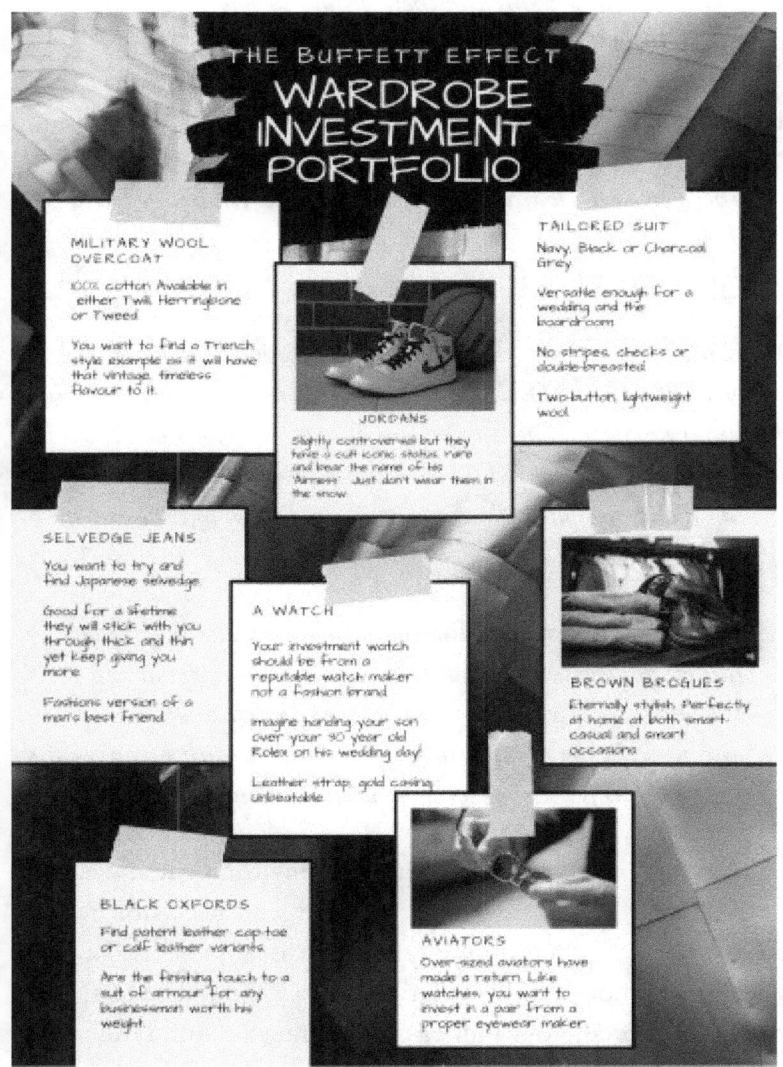

4 BUFFET INSPIRED RULES to Wardrobe Investing

1. **Keep things simple:** *To keep things simple, you need to know a good deal about them, so later in this chapter, we will look at wardrobe staple items and their history so you can spot a wonderful piece when you see one.*

1. **It must be stable and understandable:** *Buffett never invests in anything he does not understand or anything unstable. Therefore, your wardrobe investment pieces cannot be trend-driven otherwise by definition it will be out of trend soon enough, rendering it unstable.*

1. **It must have long-term prospects:** *You want to invest in pieces that will be stylish 'forever' therefore knowing your style history is important. Some menswear items have stood the test of time and have entered the 'timeless' pantheon. Much like shares in an elite company, the longer you hold them for, the greater they will reward you.*

1. **They must be undervalued:** *One of my favourite Warren Buffett quotes is; "price is what you pay, value is what you get". Like my Levi's denim suit you want to find grand pieces at a discount, the art of investing is being shrewd with resources and I prescribe this attitude for your wardrobe building.*

Fashion has a vicious consumer culture, the environment and human cost of consumerism means there is an urgent need for reform. Completely eradicating fashion consumption is impossible. I believe what's needed is a more radical evolution because fashion brings people a lot of joy, it also employs millions and is hugely important to the economies of wealthy and developing nations across the entire globe.

We, as investors in style, are not consuming, we are preserving great fashion. By shopping during sales, or finding pieces at vintage shops, charity shops, markets, or online, you stand a brilliant chance at finding great pieces for a lot less than their intrinsic value. Even Buffett himself would be proud.

Everything is designed, few things are designed well"

BRIAN REED

10. The Suit

―――

If the heart and soul of a Ferrari is the engine, the suit is the epicentre of every man's wardrobe. I say every man but we are living in an age where it is common to find guys who do not own a suit, some even scoff at the idea of wearing a suit and see it as too rigid and uncomfortable. The only thing that can make a suit too rigid and uncomfortable is the wrong suit. Before we look for ways of finding the right suit let's look at the basics starting with history.

―――――

THE ORIGINS OF THE Suit

We can trace the origins of the suit back to 18th century London, where English artisans skilled at wool fabrics were joined by foreign tailors displaced by the Napoleonic wars. Then along came **George "Beau" Brummell,** who invested his inheritance into a fighting platoon that gave him exposure to London's tailors and artisans. Brummell pioneered the notion that fabric cut and silhouette matters in male dress. He also popularized bathing once a day in warm water, much to the disparagement of society in period.

The Dandy

Known for his "stripped down" approach to dressing, his contemporaries labelled Brummell a *"Dandy"*. He is credited with delivering men from breeches into what we now know as trousers. By the mid-19th century, the frock coat gave way to a shorter jacket and trousers made of the same material. Eventually, a buttoned waistcoat styled inside the coat gave birth to the three-piece suit.

The detachable cuffs on the shirt owe their roots to the "surgeons cuffs" which the tailors on Savile Row designed to allow surgeons to roll up their sleeves and work on bleeding patients. They designed the single and double vents behind the jacket to make it comfortable to wear a coat on horseback showing how sporting activities, not just military uniform, informed the suit. The tie arrived in Britain from mainland Europe after Louis XIV was so impressed by the neckwear worn by Croatian mercenaries, hired to fight the 30 years' war. This gave birth to the cravat, a French word which is a corruption of the word Croat. The cravat arrived in Britain early in the 1800s.

American Influence

The link between the suit and work attire emerged with the rise of American business culture late in the 19th century. The American office workers wanted a compromise between the informality of the lounge suit and the regal efficiency of military uniform. From a tight row of shops behind Regent Street, the suit conquered the world. The world has changed and Saville Row has had to change too. Its core customer is no longer only royal patronage but now billionaires from Russia, China, and the Middle East.

THE ANATOMY OF THE Suit

EVERY MAN MUST OWN a Suit

The essentialness of the suit is an old-fashioned notion which has slowly been eroded by the influence of fashion and the 'dress down' corporate culture introduced in the US and increasingly becoming the 'new norm' internationally. Menswear as *fashion* has spawned varieties in the male dress, but the suit has not just survived, it has thrived. The classic man's suit is still the uniform of diplomacy, political and corporate office, keeping its intrinsic qualities of civility and trustworthiness.

Tom Ford famously said a man must have at least one timeless classic black suit. The superstar designer is not wrong there, wearing a good suit is a statement of respect for oneself but also to the world. A suit means business, it is the 'modern gentleman's armour' as quoted in the movie Kingsman. The contemporary work environment is fiercely competitive. A well-fitting suit is also irresistible to women. It is a signal to the opposite sex of success, ambition, that you can take care of business and bring the bacon home.

Contrary to the assumptions that suits are boring and rigid, the suit is a fluid and versatile choice of attire. The variations and subtle differences in suits are so exhaustive that I could write an entire book on the Jacket alone, *so let us look at the basic principles that you should know when thinking of buying your next suit.*

Bespoke

'*Be-spoken*' or '*by the customer*' the root term for bespoke; is the ultimate manifestation of a classic suit. There are over 200 components to make a traditional fully bespoke suit, each one designed and fitted to the customer's precise choices. The master-craftsmen from London's Savile Row, Milan, and across the world have kept much of the same specialist hand-making techniques and skills for well over a century.

The Bespoke Options are Endless

When buying a bespoke suit, you can choose the number of buttons, this can range from one button to five buttons or more, the consensus is that a single-breasted suit should have no more than three buttons. More on single and double-breasted options, and their splendid merits later. The options available are endless. From the fit of the shoulders, the breadth of the chest and waist, the depth of the arm, the width of the lapels to flap, jetted or patch pockets and so on.

The Fabric

The purpose of the suit will have a determining influence on the fabric. For example. If it is a work suit worn for winter months perhaps you can go for heavier wool or tweed, linen or fine cotton would be the choice if you are heading to the Caribbean to watch cricket or have semi-formal engagements in Abu Dhabi.

Buy An Extra Pair of Trousers

If you are buying a suit for extensive use, say for work, always buy two pairs of trousers. They may discontinue the Suit beyond its current season, and the trousers carry the heaviest burden of use. Most men remove their jackets while at work, yet the trousers are always in the game and are unlikely to keep their fresh appearance as long as the jacket. Buy one extra as security for your investment.

The Finisher: Waistcoat

To take it one step further is to go all the way and add a waistcoat and complete a full three-piece suit. The waistcoat just adds an extra bit of class and elegance to the overall look and is a statement of distinction and power. A waistcoat or 'vest' can be of the same fabric as the jacket and trousers but to add a dandy edge to your look it can be of a different fabric, colour or pattern. The most elegant waistcoats have five buttons and keep their lapels, however, it must marry well with the overall suit. Make sure that the textures and colours are complementary. A three-piece suit must be elegant.

Which Pocket?

We have mentioned all the above and we have not yet got to the trousers. Your tailor would ask you for a welter pocket, slanted pocket or frog pockets which bear a resemblance to a frog's mouth, further options are jetted pockets, jetted with a flap, pleats, etc. I hope I am illustrating how limitless the variations of a suit prove that it is anything but rigid and boring.

GENT NEXT DOOR

Made to Measure

As marvellous as a fully bespoke suit is, it is a luxury market. I know that a large contingent of men may not have the means or perhaps even the desire to part with a few thousand pounds for a suit. Many brands, even Savile Row tailors, offer a *'Made-to-measure'* service with their ready-to-wear collections. MTM involves taking a standard suit pattern and personalising it to the customer's request and individual measurements. The customer would still have a choice of fabrics, buttons, and pockets. The suit will be factory-made rather than at the hands of skilled tailors and cutters.

Because MTM requires less machine and handwork compared to 'full-fat' bespoke suits, they are more affordably priced. If you are looking to ease your way into the world of bespoke suiting, MTM is the way to go without spending an extensive amount of cash.

OFF THE PEG

Thankfully, modern technology advancement in automated contraction methods and understanding of the dimensions of men's bodies means that high-end suits off a *'ready to wear'* peg are of prime quality. Most menswear stores now offer regular, tailored, slim, or skinny fit suits to meet the requirements of the customer. The quality of the cut and fit may vary, mainly in conjunction with the price so it needs to be a careful but bold investment if you want a proper nice suit.

Is it A Dinner Suit or Tuxedo?

Known as a dinner suit in Britain, it was originally a derivative of the smoking jacket but cut short a few inches below the waist. A visitor to the UK took the jacket back to the US and wore it at the Tuxedo Park Club in New York, hence why it has inherited the name 'Tuxedo' Stateside. Distinguished by its satin lapels and buttons, with a satin stripe along the outer seams of the trousers. My advice is to shop around at unique brands/ retailers and see which cut you feel most comfortable in. Once you find the style and cut that work best, you can then compose your look. Buy the best your pocket can afford.

How to Conquer a 'Black Tie' Outfit

JACKET

Shawl Lapels are the smartest-looking option and have the most heritage for evening wear attire. If you want to broaden your shoulders, then go for Peak lapels.

The material of the jacket can be in traditional silk and wool blend, but a velvet option is an elegant alternative.

One button is the only way to go as it deepens the V, making you look slimmer and taller. If you go for a double-breasted jacket, then make sure it has peak lapels to give it shape.

Traditional colours are black, ivory, navy blue and burgundy. If you are feeling adventurous, go for a cherry red, or deep violet.

Never Show Your Waist

I have seen this rule broken by countless celebrities on the red carpet, and I don't like to see it. For a Black-tie event, the waist should not be on show. Wear a cummerbund or a matching waistcoat.

TROUSERS WITH 'SOME room'

Black is the way to go, ensure that they are proper evening trousers with a silk or satin stripe along the sides. It should also be self-fastening with buttons so it would not need a belt. Go for a tailored fit, you do not want them too tight and risk an embarrassing wardrobe malfunction.

Shirt

Go for a dress shirt, traditionally they come with wing-tip collars but contemporary interpretations now come with conventional collars. Dress shirts with black buttons always look more refined to me. They will also have cufflink holes, so find some nice cufflinks that are more subtle and jewellery-like because black-tie is about sophistication.

BowTie

The cherry on the cake; now I know a lot of guys would struggle to hand-tie their bowtie. I insist your bow tie be a hand-tie, why? Because you are a *GND* man, I know you will go on YouTube and spend 20 minutes learning how to do it. Not only does it look far better, but at the end of the night, you can undo it and leave it hanging around your collar. It drives the girls crazy! Thank me later.

Accessories

We have covered the cummerbund, in chapter 11, we will look further at Dress Watches. Your watch should be slim, gold or silver, with a leather strap. Ideally, it will have Roman Numerals, but under no circumstances must it be digital, that is unforgivable for a black-tie event.

You can wear a pocket square but keep it very subtle, go for a block colour, no pretentious patterns or anything too fancy.

Shoes

Velvet slippers are popular at the moment. The problem with this option is that velvet does not reflect light very well and looks dusty under lights. I would go for dress shoes with a patent finish, they can be loafers or oxfords, and must not look like shoes you can wear to work.

THE ESSENTIALS

—

11

"A gentleman's choice of watch says as much about him as does his Savile Row suit."

IAN FLEMING

11. The Essentials

The Bomber Jacket

There are some items of clothing which embody what it means to be a man, they are symbolic of timeless masculinity. The Leather Jacket is a classic gentleman's wardrobe stalwart and is perhaps the embodiment of post-war, masculine style.

Leather Jackets first appeared in the 1920s and 30s worn by fighter pilots and soldiers. They were brown goatskin style, cut at the waist with a mandarin style collar.

In the 1940s leather bomber jackets kept pilots warm in chilly cramps cockpits, the A-2, a military name afforded to the jacket lead the way.

IN WWII JACKET STYLES for pilots emerged made from horse hides and sheepskin, finished with sheep-fur collars giving birth to the now-iconic look of classic bomber jackets. Throughout history, there has always been a link between menswear and the military. The Bomber

Jacket is effectively a nickname. In the 1940s leather bomber jackets kept pilots warm in chilly cramps cockpits, the A-2, a military name afforded to the jacket lead the way.

It was of horsehide leather with a standard neck flap collar and an open zipped front. As technology advanced, WWII planes got faster meaning the pilots needed extra protection from the freezing temperatures at high altitude. So wool and fir were added and also synthetic materials were introduced such as nylon culminating ultimately with the bomber jacket leaving the military and entering public service in the mid '1950s. It quickly became a stylish choice for men who wanted a versatile jacket that could be worn from autumn right through to early spring.

The Bomber Jacket entered the limelight through Hollywood, it captured the attention of men and the imagination of women. The man affectionately known as 'The King of Cool' Steve McQueen sported a military green MA-1 Jacket in The Hunter, it later appeared on

Harrison Ford as Indiana Jones in Raiders of the Lost Ark. But without a doubt, the Bomber jacket's most famous appearance was in the 1986 classic Top Gun. Tom Cruise the ultra-cool heartthrob wore a brown A-2 leather jacket with patched badges and a synthetic (faux) fur collar. Starring as a Jet Fighter pilot it was a perfect match, a salute to the heritage of the bomber jacket and secured its status as an iconic wardrobe staple.

The Biker Jacket

The Biker Jacket stresses all the traditional masculine novelties. It squares and broadens the shoulders, then narrows towards the hip, creating the desired wedge shape.

Biker Jackets became iconic through Hollywood. Marlon Brando famously wore a Biker jacket as Johnny Strabler in the movie The Wild One.

It squares and broadens the shoulders, then narrows towards the hip, creating the desirable wedge shape.

THAT MOVIE EFFECTIVELY added the 'Biker' to the jacket, the classic squared shoulder cut, double-breasted opening with the angled YKK zip, the press button lapels and buckled leather belt became synonymous with motorcycle riders. Today designers and stylists have reinterpreted the biker, and it is now a part of contemporary outerwear for both sexes rather than just motorcycle gear for rugged male youths.

I prefer my leather jacket in Black, but bombers and bikers do also come prominently in various shades of red, grey or brown. As a stylist, I encourage my clients to invest in items of clothing that are not traditionally trend-driven, from premium or luxury brands. If you buy a biker jacket from Burberry the premium calf leather will refine and retain its quality as it gets older and will probably look great on your son in 30 years.

Timepieces

The second essential you need to have is a range of quality leather belts. I specifically mentioned quality. They don't have to be expensive but look for genuine leather or premium vegan leather. As a boy, my mother, a stylish woman in her own right, told me a woman will look for three things on a man's attire to grade his calibre. His belt, his shoes, and his watch.

You ought to wear a watch, it is an essential part of your attire. Actually, in some quarters of the business world, it is a visual clue that makes you eligible to do business with. Wearing a Rolex or Omega says you have financial clout behind you. Many people would not even do business with a man who doesn't wear a watch. To them, not wearing a watch communicates you under-appreciate both your time and the time of others. Wearing a quality men's watch is a statement of your mission, wealth, intelligence, and respectability.

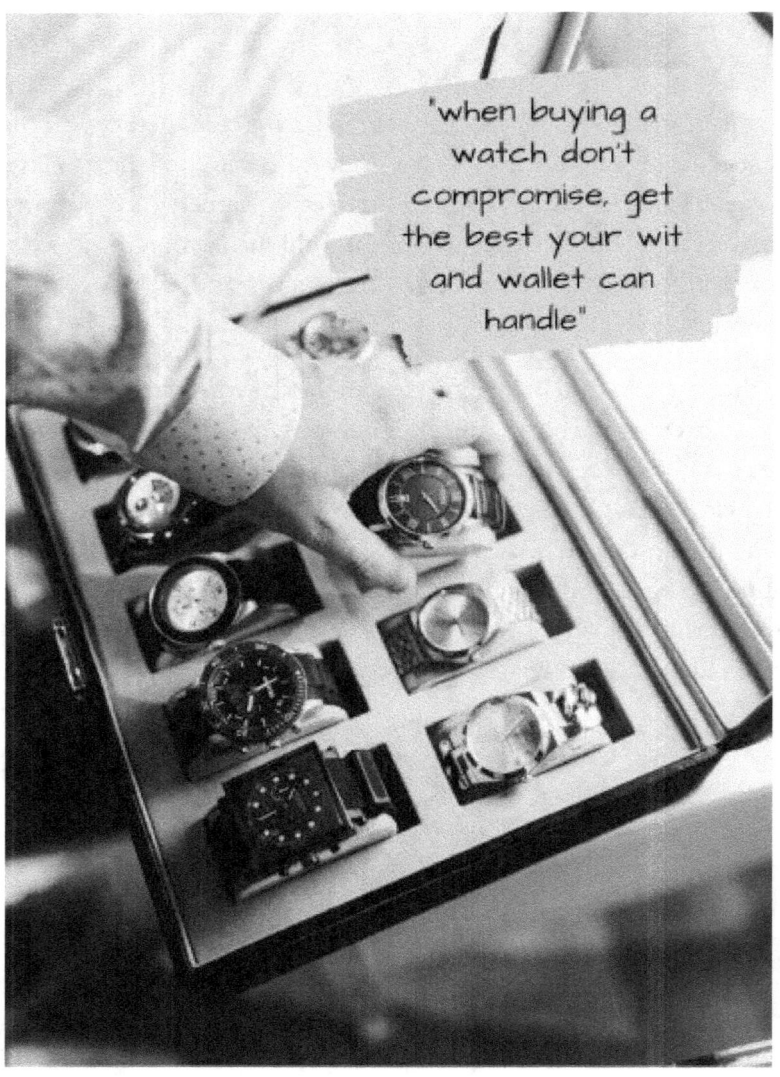

THE BASICS: WHAT YOU Must Know About Watches

Movements

The movement, also known more technically as the calibre, is how the watch ticks. It is the mechanism inside the watch that powers it. There are two main types of movement; The Quartz is the first, and it uses an oscillator which is regulated by a piece of quartz and powered by a battery. Quartz movements are relatively cheap to make, so most of the watches you would find on the high street are quartz watches.

The other principal way a watch is powered is 'Automatic'. The mechanical movement is the preferred choice for watch enthusiasts and collectors. They work by extrapolating energy from the wearer's wrists to wind the mainspring to then power the watch. Traditional powerhouse watch brands make use of automatic calibres and are predominantly all designed and made in-house. Mid-range brands would buy ready-made calibres from independent manufacturers.

What is the big deal with Automatics?

It is a little like why there is a feeding frenzy for classic sports cars such as Ferrari's or Aston Martin. A modern Golf GTI would leave a Ferrari 365 GTB/4 for dead, but while the Golf rolls out of a showroom for £30k. The legendary playboy Ferrari is exchanging hands for around £600k with the rare alloy body examples worth millions. People (men in particular) have a fascination and passion for mechanical things, and this rings true with watches.

Much like a classic car, an automatic watch has a *'soul'* it is seemingly alive and has a mystical utility to its engineering. There is no shame, however, in wearing a quartz watch despite the 'watch snobs' out there, who turn their noses up at the sight of them. Quartz watches trump automatics when it comes to accuracy *and* if you take an automatic watch off, eventually it will stop.

Types of Watches

Diving Watches

The 1953 Rolex Submariner was the first watch to work at a depth of 100 metres, giving birth to the diving watch. These watches have a roughhewn build and instructional bezel which lets divers know how much immersion time they have left.

Dress Watches

While diving watches are made with a particular usage in mind, dress watches serve no other purpose besides telling the time. They are almost as dainty as jewellery pieces and are often made of precious metal. They have a thin architecture for resting conspicuously inside the wearer's cuff. Dress watches have a 'minimum fuss' facia adorned with Roman Numerals and a leather strap.

Aviation Watches

Also known as Pilot Watches, Aviation watches owe their origins to pioneering pilots of the early twentieth century. Today, aviation watches are still a centre-piece of desire for the watch wearing fraternity. The design of the bezel and slide rule allowed these watches to give pilots a lot of vital information before electronic displays in cockpits became a thing.

Driving Watches

As we touched on earlier, there has always been a link between cars and watches. Many car enthusiasts, gentleman racers, and car collectors are watch collectors too. Much like valuable cars, collectable watches can increase in value, so are treated as assets that can be enjoyed.

Minimalist Watches

These are very popular amongst Millennials with a taste for minimalism. Minimalist watches usually use quartz movement, so they are a lot more affordable. They have simple displays and come with leather, fabric, steel, or hybrid straps.

Denim

The first traces of the jean fabric were found in the city of Genoa in the 17th Century. A major seaport and economic engine, Genoa is situated in the north-west of Italy. In Nimes, an ancient city near the coast of southern France, weavers attempted to replicate the jean fabric and produced a twill fabric with similar characteristics, but not identical to Genoa's jeans. The Nimes fabric was more fustian and understood to be of higher quality than Genoa's, which was finer and cheaper to produce.

The fabric became known as denim, derived from 'de Nimes' (*from Nimes*), Genes the French word for Genoa is the origin of the word 'jeans'. Strong fabric capable of withstanding work, the colour of choice for the denim was indigo, the dye came from India which was also where it got its name. The organic indigo from India was used until synthetic indigo was later developed in Germany.

Levi Strauss: Blue Gold

A fabric called denim became a pair of trousers or *pants* called jeans courtesy of a Bavarian-born entrepreneur called Levi Strauss. Mr Strauss left Germany for the US in 1848, ambitious and restless, Strauss heard of the Gold Rush in San Francisco and left his family in New York and moved to the West Coast.

The story goes that Mr Strauss found the miners and workers in San Francisco in need of a strong, durable fabric that could withstand the laborious demand their work entailed. Strauss imported denim from Nimes, having found the twill canvas he was using to be insufficient. He constructed the trousers in collaboration with a tailor from Reno, Nevada named Jacob Davis. Davis had written to Strauss proposing a business partnership to sell clothes reinforced with copper rivets at pressure points such as pockets and the button fly. Strauss agreed, and the duo received patent papers for *"Improvement in Fastening Pocket-Openings."* Over the ensuing years, Levi Strauss & Co experienced extraordinary success in manufacturing and selling its waist overalls to workmen across America.

THE WILD WEST & MOVIES

The 1930s ushered in an era of Western Movies depicting the West as a larger-than-life land of brave, rugged men. Catapulting the Cowboy in his Levi's denim jeans into a heroic, almost mythical icon. The idea of jeans as apparel for workmen began to erode, now becoming synonymous with the all-American man, encapsulated by stars such as Gary Cooper and John Wayne.

Post War Rebellious Youth Culture

As post-1940s wartime cultural change swept through America and the West, it invariably influenced fashion trends. Denim was now becoming prominent amongst young people and worn for leisure instead of work. On-screen heroes would appear in movies wearing jeans casually, now blue jeans on a teenager became a symbol of the excitable rebellious youth. It was during the 1950s when Levi's dropped the tag "overalls" used by its traditional customer and embraced the name *"jeans"* which was what its new customer, the leisure-loving teen called them.

WE HAVE ASSOCIATED denim with youth, rebellion, and individualism ever since.

During World War II American GI's wearing their Levi jeans could not escape the attention of admiring teens, particularly in the United Kingdom and Japan. By the 1960s, denim had made a full-fledged return to its spiritual birthplace in Europe, being received with enthusiasm by a generation of baby boomers, brimming with rebellious brashness. The interesting fact is that despite denim jeans originating from Europe they are still considered a quintessentially American staple, a notion it has kept until this day. It is also ironic that workmen wore this durable and adaptable fabric because of its functional utility at its inception. And today its additional benefits of utility, comfort, and versatility means it is still great for everyday use too.

Types of Denim

The chemicals and procedures used by denim manufacturers are intellectual property as closely guarded as a Swiss gold vault. Various chemicals and machinery are used to achieve specific characteristics, the main washes are Raw (or unwashed), Medium and Light.

Japanese Denim

Selvedge denim owes its definition to the outer-seam of the woven fabric that is made to prevent unravelling. Selvedge (self-edged) has a sturdy construction, made using old-fashioned shuttle looms which were prevalent pre-1950's. If you speak to a denim enthusiast, Japanese is the dog's testicles of all denim.

Stonewash

Light, stonewashed jeans are a nod to the original American jeans. Reliable, and long-lasting, stonewash jeans do not possess the distinctiveness or edginess of their counterparts. We find its intrinsic value in its durability, and its universal and time-honoured style.

Stretch

Contemporary and elegant, 'stretchy' denim took the world by storm in the 2010s, as skinny jeans were being adopted by Millennials as a wardrobe must-have by everyone from hipsters, rockers to prep boys. A far cry from the tough workers of old America. Thin denim has given men's jeans a narrow silhouette, although stylish they do not offer the best solution for comfort and versatility.

The various cuts and styles

Jeans come in a whole plethora of fits, cuts, and styles, determined by current trends, designers and brands. For men here are some styles to consider; *Original Fit, Slim Fit, Skinny Fit, Super Skinny, Boot Cut, Slim Boot Cut, Straights, Tapered, Athletic Fit*

We could go on and on as there are amalgamations of different fits as top brands and designers offer so much more variety these days. Rather than me talking about the merits of each cut, it would be more expedient to discuss the various elements you should consider when buying your next pair of jeans.

Body Stats

Knowing your regular jeans sizing sounds tedious, but I am always surprised at the number of men unsure of their waist size and preferred length. It is also wise to remember that brands interpret their sizing differently. Uniqlo is from Japan and will have a smaller fitting than Zara. Some brands may run a size lower for a particular season to achieve a certain look. Communicating your correct regular size to the sales assistant will enable you to pick the correct size.

Waist fit: Do you want a loose fit around your waist or do you prefer a more snug fit?

Thighs

If you are like me and have legs that resemble a long-distance track and field runner, which I would describe as slim/ athletic. I would prefer to go for regular skinny fit jeans as they give my thighs just enough curve to suggest I have some meat on my pins. Take some time to consider your thighs. Are slim, average, athletic, thick, muscular, or wide or perhaps a combination of a few of those?

Budget

Although your budget can limit what brands you can access, it will not stop you from finding a pair of jeans that will work for you. Remember what Mr Warren Buffett said *"Price is what you pay, value is what you get,"*

Belt

This is a major and underrated factor when buying jeans. If you are buying jeans for casual purposes, pair them with a thick chunky belt. Here, you need jeans with wide belt loops. If a pair of jeans is to be paired with a smart shirt or blazer, then slim loops look more elegant.

Weight

A hallmark of Japanese selvedge denim is the weight coming in at around 20 oz compared to most other denim which weighs around the 13 oz mark. Denim enthusiasts err towards heavyweight denim as it is more durable, the creases are thicker and they also offer extra protection from the elements than lighter denim.

Sunglasses

Nothing, absolutely nothing finishes a look off like the right pair of sunglasses, think of iconic images of the kings of cool such as Robert Redford, Steve McQueen, Tom Cruise, Will Smith, and David Beckham there was always a pair of shades to add a certain *'gene se quoi'* to their outfit. The eyes concealed away to add mystery to the cool, debonair exterior, leaving the beholder enough room to engage their imagination of the soul behind the stylish exterior.

So how do you go about buying 'THE' pair of sunglasses?

I did not say *a* pair of sunglasses because you can perfectly pop into your nearest chemist and secure a pair for less than five pounds. I am talking about *the* pair of sunglasses that will remind your wife of the reason she fell for your charms. The sunglasses that will make a woman fix her hair when you sit opposite her on the tube.

OK, am I the only weirdo who wears sunglasses on the underground? Anyway... I digress, let us move on.

What to consider: Face Shape

We touched on body shape and discussed the influence it has on our sartorial choices; sunglasses sit on our face and not our bodies. Likewise, our faces also have unique shapes, so we also have to consider this when choosing a pair of sunglasses.

Oval

What the hourglass is to women, and the Trapezoid is for men, is what the Oval face shape is to you. Your face is taller than it is wider t, you have the enviable burden of being able to wear any shaped frames and pull it off. It means you will spend a fair amount of time trying on various pairs but you are highly unlikely to make a poor decision when you finally land THE pair!

GND recommends Classic Aviators with a full-frame or Wayfarer frames preferably Ray Bans but any top brand will do.

Round

Round face shape is when the height and width of your face are roughly similar. This shape favours defined, geometric shaped frames that lengthen the face.

GND recommends: Classic Ray-Bans with the Wayfarer shape make a superb choice, Square Aviators, and Clubmaster/ Browline are also cool frames with geometric architecture.

Square

Great! You probably have distinctive chiselled jaws ala Brad Pitt with strong cheekbones. To strengthen your features, ironically we soften the shape of the frames, opting for curves and round frames.

GND recommends: Teardrop aviators or vintage round frames would stress your jawline, another great option for square faces is semi-rimmed frames

Heart

Typically distinguished by a broader brow and a chin that is narrower in comparison is the heart shape. To add balance to your proportions, opt for lenses with a lighter shade/tint and low-profile frames, this will elongate your face as attention is diverted downwards.

GND recommends Classic Aviators, Wrap-round Rectangle, and rectangle frameless frames.

Hats

Several years ago, I designed a collection inspired by the spaghetti westerns which I used to watch as a boy. During the creative process, a particular image was most prominent in my mind. It was Clint Eastwood's iconic poncho over jeans look featured in *'A Fistful of Dollars, and A Few Dollars More'* and most famously in *'The Good, The Bad and The Ugly'*. The poncho gave him a sense of strength and mystery. It was a shield against his enemies but also concealed his weapon, hiding his strength. Pondering on that image a little more, what topped it off was his hat, the iconic wide-brimmed brown hat made from beaver skin resting on his head like a crown. A hat is usually the last thing a man puts on as he is about to leave and face the world. It is the cherry on the cake or the artist's signature. The hat you wear and how you wear it does not just reveal your taste, but also a little about your personality.

Part of becoming a stylish person and establishing an original signature style is taking time to understand your clothes, and in this case, hats.

As much as watches are a feat of engineering and suits are a work of craftsmanship, hats are a work of art.

YOU MUST KNOW CONCLUSIVELY the name of your hat, its functional and sartorial benefits, and the history and tradition behind it. Only when you understand the rules, can you then bend or break them to bring your originality.

Remember the art of dressing well is about proportion and illusions, we want to stress those areas that are most attractive about us.

Hats for the larger Gent

Men with larger heads suit larger hats with a wide brim, a hat with small brim will only make everything look larger and less elegant. Instead, a larger brim will bring everything into more even proportion. You also want a broad wrap band and a medium to the large-sized crown.

Vintage Fedora   Modern Homburg

Brim depth: 2.5 inches/ 6.25cm minimum GND recommends: Fedora, Homburg, Cowboy

Hats for the Short, Slim & Medium Gent

If you are shorter in stature, you immediately gain height by wearing a hat as it elongates your body. Narrow brim hats suit men with smaller heads. Naturally, there are exceptions, but that is generally how it works. It also helps to have your rim curled up rather than snapped, which gives the viewer the perception of elevation and height.

Vintage Bowler   Modern Trilby

Brim depth: 2 in or 5 cm maximum GND recommends - Trilby, Porkie-pie, Bucket, Bowler.

GENT NEXT DOOR

Fedora

I recall spending an evening with my mother looking through some old black and white photographs. One photo, in particular, stands out in my memory, it was of my grandfather, he must have been in his mid-twenties in 1940's Zimbabwe (or Rhodesia back then). He was dressed in a grey, very sharp suit. He also had on a fedora hat, topping off a classic look made famous or perhaps infamous by the ludicrously well-dressed mobsters of that era.

Fedora started Life as a Ladies Hat

"Fedora" was a play by French author Victorien Sardou, the play tells the story of Princess Fedora Romanoff played by the actress Sarah Bernhardt. In it, she wore a soft-brimmed hat that quickly became popular amongst women. It was not until Prince Edward was pictured in a Fedora in 1924 that it became a fashion for men.

AL CAPONE & THE MOB

When infamous mob leader Al Capone's mugshot captured him wearing a Fedora, it quickly became associated with prohibition, glamorising the gangster lifestyle in the 1920s and 30s. Typically, Hollywood would play a key role in the popularisation of the Fedora with Humphrey Bogart wearing a Fedora in 'Casablanca'. Brian De Palma's 1987 gangster film 'The Untouchables', which tells the story of prohibition agent Eliot Ness played by Kevin Costner and his pursuit of Al Capone portrayed by Robert De Niro. The masterful Giorgio Armani dressed the stars in pinstripe suits while costume designer Marilyn Vance donned the men on both sides of the law in felt, wide-brim Fedora hats.

The Fedora's Cousin

The Fedora is distinguished by its pinched front on either side, creating a crease on its crown. Traditionally made of soft felt but also fashioned in twill, wool, velvet, and suede. The brim is wide. This is an important detail that distinguishes a Fedora from a Trilby which has a narrow brim. Do not make the mistake of buying a Trilby hat when you are looking for a Fedora. The Trilby is more common and in my humble opinion not as sophisticated and stylish as a Fedora.

Homburg

Originally from Germany, the Homburg hat has a crown which is distinctly higher than a fedora's. The brim is wide with a gentle upward curve round. It is an elegant hat, one that speaks of a gentleman with actual class and pedigree. In the contemporary menswear scope, it is less common than other felt hats. This is a magnificent hat to own if you like to stand out

It burst onto the fashion scene in the late 1800s after a certain Prince Edward VII (who else?) Visited Bad Homburg, near Frankfurt, Germany. They published a photograph of the Prince holding a

Homburg in Harper's Weekly and the hat's popularity catapulted. Favoured as a more comfortable and versatile alternative to the Top hat amongst the elite of British society. This is traditionally a hat for the distinguished gentleman, it evokes power and understated opulence, and it looks great over a suit or an overcoat.

Panama

A curious case if ever there was one. The highly celebrated Panama Hat lends its name to the Panamanian men who worked on the isthmus that links North and South America. The men wore the graceful fibre hats for protection from the piercing equatorial sun and affectionately named the hats after their homeland rather than the country of its manufacture, Ecuador. Fibres took from Paja Toquilla plants found in the coastal regions of Ecuador to create the hats.

The evocative style and superior quality of Panama hats swiftly discovered and embraced in the United States in the 18th century. Theodore Roosevelt famously wore it on a visit to Panama, in France, the young Napoleon III was a wearer of Panama hats and in England, it crowned the head of the finest dandies of influential society. Today we still see it as the ultimate summer hat, particularly in England. A sea of straw-coloured Panama's at sporting events such as Wimbledon, Henley Royal Regatta, and the Lord's Test Match is one of the glorious spectacles of a British summer.

Boater

If Panama is the Nutella of summer hats, then the Boater is the marmite. I understand the boater hat to be a derivative of the flat-topped caps worn by French sailors.

The Boater originated from Bedfordshire, England; it was fashioned from plaited straw coiled together then moulded into its distinctive flat pillbox shape

and a flat brim, then encircled by a red and blue ribbon.

The Boater has been on an inconstant journey for 150 years, as a result, it polarises opinion. For me, it is a symbol of sartorial elegance (think

Great Gatsby), but for many, the association with girl's school uniform is a turnoff. In the 19th century, its popularity dwindled, being eclipsed by Panama hats and by Trilby hats in the early 20th century. The boater's nautical ancestry has meant it is an affectionate mainstay at Henley Royal Regatta, other popular associations include barbershop quartets and jazz bands.

Flat Cap

To preserve the prosperity of the wool industry, the British government decreed a 1571 act of parliament that all males over the age of 6 years would wear flat caps of wool manufacture on Sundays and holidays, with the notable exception of noble persons or persons of degree. As odious as this sounds, the bill was not revoked for almost 30 years. As a result, the flat cap became synonymous with the

working-class. I must point it out that this stereotype is erroneous as gentlemen of high society would sport flat caps in the countryside. Hence why it is commonly referred to as a 'golf cap'. The flat cap and its close cousin the 'Peaky' has seen an unprecedented return in popularity because of the cult streaming TV show Peaky Blinders. The period based drama has informed men's winter fashion trends with more men wanting to dress smarter.

Footwear

Interview: Franklin Boateng aka King of Trainers

To some, the cult-like world of sneaker culture can be difficult to understand, so I called upon Franklin Boaten. An expert who has lived and breathed the culture all his life, to help us understand.

For someone who wants to get involved in sneaker culture and start a collection, what advice would you give them?

If you want to get into the collecting culture or enthusiast culture, the first thing is, it's not about getting into it, you kind of already have to love it.

For me it's not about "getting into" something, I was born loving the trainers so you should

already have a love for it and then you can expand on that love.

I would recommend you to buy what you like and not follow the 'hype' of the crowd. It is harder when starting your collection to get hype trainers unless you've got a lot of money. So just buy what you like and enjoy it. Enjoyment is the main thing!

How would you define true sneaker enthusiasts?

A true sneaker enthusiast is someone who loves what they love, not what everyone loves. The hype and the media drive you to like certain things and I admit to having been sucked into it before but at the end of the day, I buy what I love. I pass on a lot of hype shoes because I have very little care for them so it's important to just buy what you love and that for me is a true enthusiast.

Most guys are familiar with the big brands like Nike, Adidas, Jordans etc. Are there any boutique or emerging brands we should look out for?

There are so many good brands, I grew up wearing Nike in particular, Adidas, Reebok, etc but now I wear everything. My favourite brand at the moment is Ellesse, they are doing some amazing things and they are a heritage brand and have been around for a while. Diadora as well who are excellent, these would be called boutique brands as they may not have the same international presence as the mainstream brands. If I am honest they make better quality trainers, that's just facts. I have been to Diadora's factory and it's a proper facility. Their quality is the best.

I have my collaboration with Ellesse; it is called DECADE, and it is dedicated to my mother. It is me taking the Ellesse shoe called the Tanker and flipping it with inspiration from Boris Becker's Wimbledon win in 85. He was wearing a light blue and dark blue Tennis jacket and I took those colours and put them on my trainers. You can have a look at them online for more!

Tell us a bit about King of trainers. How did it all start?

So my name is Franklin Boateng, my nickname is King of Trainers and it's all come from that era in 1985. When I was growing up we never had much, it was one pair of shoes and trainers per year and that's all you had. My mum loved tennis and everything about it so when Boris Becker won that Wimbledon championship my mum would look at everything tennis players wore and thought 'this must be good', tennis was the ultimate sport back then.

So my mum bought me the Puma's and Reeboks from tennis and I was the only one with them at infant school. So King of Trainers was a nickname from   back   then

when I was a kid and then this has translated to me being a personality online.

I now have the only footwear award show that is voted by the public, I do various things in the sneaker community from exhibitions and events to sharing information and stories. I am also a consultant and have probably consulted for every footwear brand out there and work with a lot of them. For someone who grew up loving trainers, I am living my dream of being able to work in the industry.

How can people connect with your movement?

*I call my followers The Kingdom so can follow me on Instagram **@kingoftrainers** I reply to people on DM if you leave a comment I respond. It is just about connecting with people so 90% of the time I will respond.*

*On a business level, you can check me out **@franklinboateng** feel free to google me. I have done a lot of things in the business world such as social media management, lecturing, Ted Talks etc.*

Thanks, Tinashe, enjoy the book, everyone!

Franklin aka King of Trainers.

Sports Shoes & Culture

The world of trainers or sneakers as they are known in North America has come a long from the early twentieth century. Perhaps history's most famous story of brotherly enmity is of the Dassler's from Germany. The Dassler Brothers Sports Shoe company made the world's best sports shoes in the 1930s. Their shoes were famously worn by Jesse Owens at the Berlin Olympic Games and as a result, the popularity of their shoes exploded. Despite their success, the brothers could not separate their differences to the point where they ended the company shortly after World War 2 and in 1949 Adolf 'Adi' formed Adidas and Rudolf started Puma. These two companies have gone on to be dominant forces of sportswear since but both still have their headquarters in the same Bavarian town. Although both brothers are now passed, the brands are still sworn enemies.

His "Airness"

In 1984 Nike signed a rookie basketball player by the name of Michael Jordan. It was seen by many as a speculative investment in such an unproven talent, but clearly, someone at Nike had done their due diligence because few who followed college basketball in the early 1980s would have known that 'Mike' Jordan as he was known in college was going to change the sport forever. In 1985 the first-ever Air Jordan's were launched, and the rest, as they say, is history.

Why Must You Own a Pair of Jordans

Air Jordans are a moment in history for sports shoes, and for fashion. Michael Jordan himself is a moment in history, further emphasised by the brilliant Netflix documentary *The Last Dance*. Owning a pair of Jordans is buying into that moment, capturing some of the mystique around Michael Jordan. A crisp pair from the early 90s is probably the sweet spot as they were rarer, and the build quality is superior to the modern Jordans. Paying a premium for vintage pairs is a reasonable expectation, but they are likely to increase in value, anyway. As a wardrobe investment, Air Jordans tick every box of our criteria.

Hip-Hop & Footwear

Another seismic moment for trainers was when some Adidas executives were invited to a hip-hop concert in New York. A group called Run DMC had made a hit song called *'My Adidas',* on hearing the capacity crowd rap along word-for-word, the Adidas cheque book joined the party and signed Run DMC to an endorsement contract. This was a watershed moment as for the first time it was sports shoes crossing over into culture, fashion, and music simultaneously.

Trainers are now such an integral part of fashion and exclusive sneakers being voraciously sought after like a Steve Jobs era iPhone. All the major fashion houses have their line of trainers either designed in house or in some form of collaboration. Rappers such as Kid Cudi (Guiseppe Zanotti), A$AP Rocky (Under Armour), and most prominent of all Kanye West with his Yeezy Boosts have their trainer lines which sell out within hours of release.

FINDING
INSPIRATION

—

12

"We are called to be
architects of the
future, not its victims"

BUCKMINSTER FULLER

12. Finding Inspiration

———

Inspiration - Derived from the Latin word 'inspirare' the verb inspire defined "fill (someone) with the urge or ability to do or feel something, especially to do something creative"

We came to an understanding earlier that personal style is an art, we have explored some of the more technical elements to dressing well such as colour and proportion. These are important elements that encourage us to think correctly about our sartorial approach. Once we have these skills it is no longer about analysing, it is time to feel. Being stylish is more than a skill or a technique, it is a feeling, it is something that you are inspired to do, so let us look at ways to find compelling inspiration.

MoodBoarding

When a client hires me to style their campaign shoot or editorial, I use a corkboard in my home office to visually display what is inspiring my ideas for the coming shoot. Taking cutouts from magazines, books, look books, newspapers, or whatever else I come across, I pin these visual clues onto my corkboard. At first view, it is a chaotic mess but with closer viewing, a pattern emerges like a juxtaposed jigsaw puzzle. The mood board acts as a reference point that I can always return to at any stage of the shoot. It reminds me of the story I want to tell through the clothes I am dressing the model or client in.

Have a Vision & Write it Down

In a recent study, a professor at Virginia Tech uncovered some rather interesting facts. He surveyed a large group of people and asked: *"What are your life goals for your life?"* Below are his findings.

- 80% of Americans said they did not have life goals.

- 16% had never written them down.

- 4% had written their goals down but never looked at them again.

- 1% had written their goals and looked at them regularly.

Which of this group of folks are high achievers?

Yes of course.. the one percent group!

"Write the vision, and make it plain on tables, that he who reads it may run." - Habakkuk 2:2

CREATING YOUR STYLE Mood board

We explored earlier how your purpose, your mission, and your archetype are all essential elements of your style. Your style mood board is a visual way of interpreting those three key pillars of personality wholeness. You can create a physical mood board at home and mount it up on your bedroom wall. Each morning take a moment and can glance at it when composing your outfit for the day. Add a digital mood board which you can create using apps like Canva on your smartphone or laptop. This will serve as your secret pocket stylist, refer to it when shopping around town or shopping online.

FINDING STYLE INSPIRATION
MUST WATCH FILMS & SHOWS

FOR WORK & BUSINESS
- Wall Street Money Never Sleeps
- SUITS
- Kingsmar
- White Colar

FOR EDGY FUTURISM
- The Matrix Reloaded
- Black Panther
- The Fifth Element

FOR SARTORIAL SPLENDOUR
- The Talented Mr Ripley
- The Great Gatsby (2013)
- Grand Hotel Budapest

FOR THE 90'S OPTIMISM
- Clueless
- Saved by the Bell
- Kids
- Beverly Hills 91210

FOR URBAN ATTITUDE
- Straight Outta Compton
- Boys in the Hood
- The Wood

FOR SWAGGER & CONFIDENCE
- The Thomas Crown Affair (1999)
- Iron Man
- SUITS
- 300
- Anchorman
- Top Gun
- The Good The Bad & The Ugly
- Shaft

FOR THAT 80'S COOL
- Miami Vice (orignal)
- Fame (1980)
- Wild Style (1983)
- Ferris Beuler's Day Off
- Top Gun

FOR RETRO REVIVAL
Peaky Blinders
The Get Down
The Great Gatsby (1964)
Live & Let Die

---

4 STEPS TO CREATING *Your Style Moodboard*

Analogue Vision Board - *Cork Board, pins, scissors, and some Pritt stick glue.*

Digital Vision Board - *Smartphone, Tablet, or Laptop computer. Apps to use are Pinterest, Canva.*

1, Click & Collect

Allow your eyes to wonder at the images that inspire, delight, and intrigue you. Magazine tear-offs, Newspaper cutouts, buttons, belt buckles, pins or badges, fabrics, photographs. Physical examples can be found anywhere from your parent's garage, loft, or basement to charity shops, vintage fairs, and boot sales. Digital examples can be found by simply typing in keywords into a google search or my personal favourite the search option on Pinterest.

2. Style & Compile

Piecing together your mood board is not necessarily something that you can do in one sitting on a Sunday afternoon. After over 15 years as a creative professional one thing I can say confidently is that creativity and ideas cannot be forced, true creativity is usually the result of instinctive and often impulsive moments. So compiling a really good mood board could and really should take a few days or even weeks. You could be at the train station and spot something on a billboard and you decide to take a snap on your smartphone. It could be a photo of a beautiful piece of architecture which caught your eye from a magazine at the reception lounge desk. It can come from anywhere.

3. Allow your imagination to run

Avoid thinking too long and hard about it. Every time you come across something that has an element in line with your style vision, cut it out, cut it off and add it to your compilation. Don't be embarrassed early on, while your mood board is taking shape it can look awkward and confused. Just keep going and you will surprise yourself with the nuggets of inspiration your mind will come alive too.

4. Seeing is Believing:

We have all heard the term *"out of sight out of mind"* it is one of those truisms of life. As humans, we are moved by what we see, if you doubt that just consider the astronomical advertising budgets companies reserve for a 30-second commercial during the Super Bowl every year. They do this in the strong conviction that the visuals they will parade in front of the millions of watching eyes will inspire them to part with their hard-earned cash. These companies understand the power of imagery. Remember those 1 percenters from earlier in this chapter? The message is clear, keep your vision before your eyes.

As I suggested earlier you may want to hang up the corkboard displaying your wonderful artistic work somewhere in your bedroom so you can gaze at it each morning. You can put in at the base of your staircase or even by your breakfast table. If you have gone the digital route, a simple and quick solution is to screenshot your mood board and leave it as a screensaver on your laptop or smartphone. Look at the vision board every day. Much like the mood board I created for my photoshoots, it will become like a

recipe book for your wardrobe. Providing you with some inspirational flair for hot date outfits, a Drake concert at the O2, or a networking branch.

Begin With the End in Mind

Your vision board will help make sure that you are never stuck for idea or direction, it will include the colours that match your skin tone, shapes, and images that refer to your body shape and pictures of things that are in line with who you are and where you are aspiring to go in life. I encourage you to go ahead and create it even if you don't see yourself as a particularly creative or artistic person. This ought to be a fun and liberating process, and remember if you do not have a vision of where you want to go, it is unlikely you will go anywhere.

For how long do I keep my mood board?

For as long as it takes to get fully immersed in your style archetype. Your style vision board is not static, it is an ever-evolving almost organic thing, you will get into the habit of finding inspiration from all sorts of places. Perhaps you will find an artefact at a flea market in Marrakech and think it is perfect to add onto your style mood board. Its shade of colour or texture can influence the choice of tie you purchase. Do you see how incredibly useful and fun this can be?

Go ahead let your imagination run free!

About the Author

———

Tinashe Dennis Immanuel started his fashion career as a designer, setting up his first clothing line with a university friend, which led him to spread his creative wings further into styling. His Fashion Styling credits spread from published editorials, commercials and Television. Affectionately known as 'Dennis' in the industry, he has designed costumes and wardrobe for short and feature-length films.

———

TINASHE DENNIS IMMANUEL

Tinashe Dennis Immanuel is also an entrepreneur, tutor and visiting lecturer at several Universities and Colleges in England.

Instagram - gentnextdoor

www.gentnextdoor.com[1]

Acknowledgements

A SPECIAL THANKS TO:

John Gyeni and John Junior Ampen for inspiring me to design clothes in my dorm room at university and being a continual source of motivation throughout the years. To Junior Agyeman for always being my rear gunner and for your stunning photography featured so prominently in this book.

To my siblings Tendai, Sean and Tonderai Immanuel for your support along the way.

Arthur Sempebwa for giving me the space to finish this book in your home and allowing me to use your MacBook pro.

Franklin Boateng for the interview within the book. Thanks for your generosity and acumen, bro.

To all the photographers and illustrators who contributed their images to this book.

To all the remarkable creative professionals I have worked with during my 15 years in the fashion and entertainment space.

To all my friends, too many to name, but I appreciate you all. To my GCSE design teacher Mr Giles for being a pivotal male role model and positive influence at a crucial age.

And lastly to God and to my late mother Elizabeth Immanuel, thank you for having unwavering confidence in me and for raising me to be a gentleman. Your memory is like a reassuring embrace that gives me strength, I dedicate this book to you.

PHOTO CREDITS

Front Cover fashion flat lay: pexels.com

Chapter images: Junior Agyeman, modelling and styling by Tinashe Dennis Immanuel

Photo 1: Rise of Mens Fashion, photo by Junior Agyeman

Photo 2: Black Queen Chess Piece by George Becker via pexels.com

Photo 3: Oh lala Chapter Image by P C; pexels.com

Photo 4: love couple photo by cotton bro; pexels.com

Photo 5: Man in red blazer by Fikayo Aderoju on Pexels.com

Photo 6: Man in all black Photo by Pedram Normohamadian on Unsplash

Photo 7: Man in Gym gear Photo by Alexander Redl on Unsplash

Photo 8: Row of Suits Photo by David Bartus on Pexels.com

Photo 9: Pink Blazer Photo by Heng Films on Unsplash

Photo 10: Sports Jackets Photo by Alexander Naglestad on Unsplash

Photo 11: Man in white casual shirt Photo by Marius Muresan on Unsplash

Photo 12: Row of Smart Suits Pixabay on Pexels.com

Photo 13: Man in Double-breasted suit Photo by Clem Onojeghuo on Unsplash

Photo 14: Man in Single-breasted suit Photo by Steffen Wienberg on Unsplash

Photo 15: Pocket SquarePhoto by Tyler Harris on Unsplash, Cufflinks Photo by Nate Johnston on Unsplash, Men in Socks Spanwire on Pexels.com

Photo 16: Monk Strap Shoes Photo by Jia Ye on Unsplash, Penny Loafers Photo by Jeroen den Otter on Unsplash

Photo 16: Brown Brogues Photo by Matthew Feeney on Unsplash, Brown Oxfords Photo by Terje Sollie from Pexels

Photo 17: Tinashe Dennis Immanuel in Biker Jacket Photo by @justplain_e

Photo 18: Brown wooden puppet running, pixabay

Photo 19, 20, 21: Types of male figure illustrations, adobe stock

Photo 22: Gold & Silver keys, coins and ornaments Photo by Madison Inouye from Pexels

Photo 23, 24, 25: Man in Skin Undertone images Photos by @justplain_e

Photo 26: Nativity Painting, pixabay

Photo 27: The Classic man Photo by Javier Reyes on Unsplash

Photo 28: The Melodramatic man Photo by Jacobwithu on Unsplash

Photo 29; The Utility Man Photo by Ian Keefe on Unsplash

Photo 30: The Romantic Man Photo by Mariya Georgieva on Unsplash

Photo 31: The Impish Man Photo by Nathan Dumlao on Unsplash

Photo 32: The Boyish Man Photo by Clem Onojeghuo on Unsplash

Photo 33: The Drip Man Photo by Gabriel Côté on Unsplash

Photo 34: Man searching on apparels photo by Matt Hardy via pexels.com

Photo 35: Air Jordan on infographic photo by JD Danny via pexels.com

Photo 36: Brown wingtip shoes on infographic photo by Terje Sollie via pexels.com

Photo 37: Person holding aviator sunglasses on infographic photo by Andrea Piacquadio via pexels.com

Photo 38: Anatomy of the Suit Photo by Junior Agyeman

Photo 39: Bespoke Tailor Photo by SinAbrochar on Unsplash

Photo 40: Doppelganger Suit Shop Photo mino21 - stock.adobe.com

Photo 41: Man in a two-piece suit photo by Malcolm Garrett via pexels.com

Photo 42: Suit Shop interior Photo by Jozsef Hocza on Unsplash

Photo 43: Man in White Dinner Suit Pixabay on Pexels.com

Photo 44: Man in Car in Dinner Suit Photo by OSPAN ALI on Unsplash

Photo 45: Man in aviator pilot gear from Adobe Stock

Photo 44: Man in modern A2 Bomber Jacket Photo by Prince Akachi on Unsplash

Photo 45: Man in Biker Jacket Photo by Tyler Nix on Unsplash

Photo 46: Box of Watched photo by Mister Mister, pexels.com

Photo 47: Diving Watch Photo by John Torcasio on Unsplash 48: Dress Watch photo by Philip Lindvall, pexels.com Photo 49: Aviation Watch Photo by Frank Park on Unsplash Photo 50:

GENT NEXT DOOR

Driving Watch pixabay via pexels.com Photo 51: Minimalist Watch photo by Luca Nardone, pexels.com

Photo 51: Levi's Shirt Photo by K8 on Unsplash

Photo 52: Man in jeans by Malcolm Garret; pexels.com

Photo 53: Man in sunglasses Photo by Hannah Reding on Unsplash

Photo 54, 55, 56, 57: Face shape illustrations; shutterstock.com

Photo 58: Man wearing a hat photo by C.O; pexels.com

Photo 59: Fedora and Homburg hats; Shutterstock

Photo 60: Bowler and Trilby hat; Shutterstock

Photo 61: Man in Fedora Photo by ZACHARY STAINES on UnsplashPhoto

62: Man in Panama Hat photo by Malcolm Garrett; pexels.com

Photo 63: Man in a Boater Hat Photo by Chi Lok TSANG on Unsplash

Photo 64: Man in a Flat cap photo by nappy; pexels.com

Photo 65, 66: Franklin Boateng aka King of Trainers in a Suit photos by @Lovo_jimbo

Photo 67: Air Jordans Photo by Hunter Johnson on Unsplash

Photo 68: Man in inspiration mood board Photo by Junior Agyeman

Photo 69: Photo of Kitchen Table Photo by Daria Shevtsova on pexels.com

Photo 70: Photo of Tinashe Dennis Immanuel by Grant Ritchie

Don't miss out!

Visit the website below and you can sign up to receive emails whenever Tinashe Dennis Immanuel publishes a new book. There's no charge and no obligation.

https://books2read.com/r/B-A-MWDL-ICOGB

BOOKS 2 READ

Connecting independent readers to independent writers.